The 1066 Country Walk
By Nick Brown

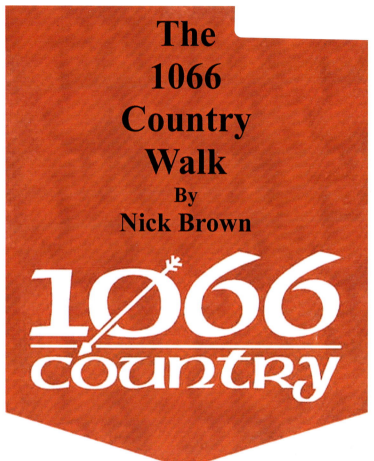

First published in Great Britain in 2011 by Trailguides Limited.
www.trailguides.co.uk

ISBN 978-1-905444-45-8

All rights reserved. No part of this publication may be reproduced, stored in a retrieval system, or transmitted in any form or by any means (electronic, mechanical photocopying, recording or otherwise), without the written permission of Trailguides Limited.

Copyright © 2011 Nick Brown

**Trailguides Limited
35 Carmel Road South
Darlington
Co Durham DL3 8DQ**

Cover design by Steve Gustard

CONTENTS

	Page
INTRODUCTION	
1. Introduction to the 1066 Country Walk	4
2. The 1066 Country Walk – description and statistics	4
3. The Walks	6
4. The Maps	7
5. Tourist Information Centres & Websites	7
6. Public Transport	8
7. Accommodation	8
8. Pubs and Tea Rooms on the 1066 route	9
9. 1066 Feeder Links to Bexhill & Hastings	9
10. Long Distance Footpath links	10
11. FAQs	11
12. 1066 Battle of Hastings – background	12
13. The Countryside Code	12
THE WALKS	
The 1066 Country Walk	
Stage 1. Pevensey Castle to Boreham Street 7.42 miles	16
Stage 2. Boreham Street to Ashburnham 2.68 miles	23
Stage 3. Ashburnham to Battle Abbey 6.60 miles	27
Stage 4. Battle Abbey to Westfield 4.90 miles	33
Stage 5. Westfield to Icklesham 4.90 miles	39
Stage 6. Icklesham to Rye 5.62 miles	46
Circular Walks on the 1066 route	
Walk 1. Herstmonceux 5.80 miles	54
Walk 2. Battle Abbey 5.70 miles	59
Walk 3. Westfield 4.90 miles	66
Walk 4. Broad Street, Icklesham 4.50 miles	72
Walk 5. Icklesham 5.00 miles	77
Walk 6. Rye 4.25 miles	83
APPENDIX	
The Author	88
Walking South East	89
Acknowledgements	90
Disclaimer	90

INTRODUCTION

1. Introduction to The 1066 Country Walk

In September 1066 William Duke of Normandy brought his army to Pevensey in East Sussex, and went on to defeat King Harold at the Battle of Hastings, thus changing the course of English history forever. You can follow in the footsteps of William the Conqueror taking in such historical gems as Pevensey Castle, Herstmonceux Castle, world famous Battle Abbey, the medieval town of Winchelsea and the unique charms of Rye. The 1066 Country Walk goes through some absolutely glorious countryside containing picturesque villages, quaint hamlets, Anglo-Saxon and Norman churches, oast houses, windmills, ancient woodland, rivers and breathtaking valleys.

For the first time the 1066 Country Walk is broken down into 6 separate stages by local author Nick Brown, each with its own sketch map, superb photos and interesting snippets of local history. In addition his detailed guide to refreshments, accommodation, public transport, useful websites and FAQs provides walkers with all the essential information they will require when planning their itinerary. In addition there are 6 circular walks in the second half of the book, all incorporating part of the 1066 route, which allows walkers to explore even more of this delightful countryside!

2. The 1066 Country Walk – description and statistics

This is a fairly easy, generally low level walk which starts at Pevensey Castle in East Sussex and goes via Battle, where William the Conqueror defeated King Harold of England, to finish at Rye. It makes for an ideal long distance walking weekend, with a suggested overnight stop either at Battle (which is just past the halfway point) or at my local village of Westfield (which leaves just 10.50 miles to be covered on the final day). There are good rail links to Pevensey, Battle and Rye which makes this easily accessible to walkers based in London and the Home Counties.

According to my Garmin Forerunner 405 watch, the actual distance is 32.12 miles; slightly longer than the 31 miles which has been generally accepted for aeons! There is nothing even remotely taxing in the opening two stages, which makes Tent Hill on Stage 3 quite a shock to the system! Stage 4 has some gentle undulations through Battle Great Wood; and then there are three stiff climbs in Stage 5 between Westfield and Icklesham. Stage 6 is relatively easy, allowing you to enjoy some magnificent views across to the English Channel and also down into the Brede Valley.

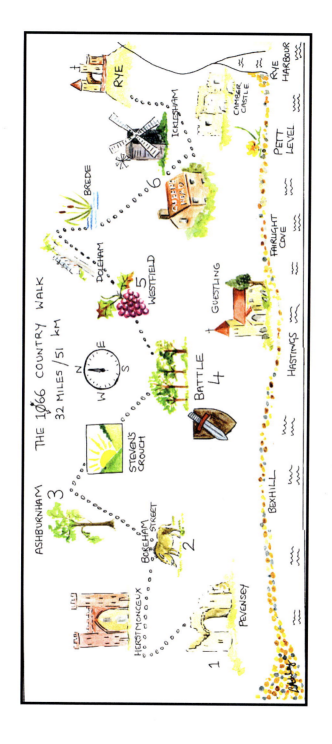

Copyright © Lorraine Ashley.

- Total distance 32.12 miles (51.70 kms)
- Total ascent 2061 ft (628 metres)
- Total descent 2096 ft (639 metres)
- Maximum elevation 381 ft (116 metres) at the top of Tent Hill
- 58% off road paths; 17% off road hard track (rural); 20% quiet lanes/private and unmade roads; 5% main road (pavement, some grass verge)
- STAGES 1 – 3 16.70 miles (26.88 kms); ascent 1201 ft (366 metres); descent 977 ft (298 metres)
- STAGES 4 – 6 15.42 miles (24.82 kms); ascent 860 ft (262 metres); descent 1119 ft (341 metres)

3. The Walks

- Walks are graded for degree of difficulty, ranging from 1 (Easy) to 5 (Very testing!)
- Dog walkers are advised on each route as to the likelihood of encountering sheep, cows and other livestock
- Superb photos accompany each route; additional photos can be accessed on the book's website www.spanglefish.com/1066countrywalk
- Easy to follow sketch maps drawn by Westfield artist Lorraine Ashley
- All routes measured using a Garmin Forerunner 405 watch
- Fascinating pieces of local history permeate each route
- Just two maps are needed to cover all the walks – full details provided on

each individual walk
- Full details also provided for parking, public transport and refreshments
- Useful website links also provided on each walk

4. The Maps

Virtually all the six stages of The 1066 Country Walk are covered by Ordnance Survey Explorer Map 124 Hastings & Bexhill. The final ½ mile to the finish at Rye is covered by OS Explorer Map 125 Romney Marsh, Rye & Winchelsea; however this section is so easy to follow that it doesn't warrant buying the extra map! Similarly all six circular walks are covered by OS Map 124, excepting no. 6 Rye where the first ½ mile and final mile fall into OS Map 125 territory; again though this is so straightforward to follow that you don't really need to purchase the additional map!

5. Tourist Information Centres & Websites

Within the 1066 area there are three main Tourist Information Centres based at Battle, Hastings and Rye. Contact details are as follows:

Battle Tourist Information Centre
Battle Abbey, Gatehouse, Battle, East Sussex TN33 OAD
Tele: 01424 776789
Website: battletic@rother.gov.uk

Hastings Tourist Information Office
Queens Square, Hastings, East Sussex TN34 1TL
Tele: 01424 451111
Website: hic@hastings.gov.uk

Rye Tourist Information Centre
4 – 5 Lion Street, Rye, East Sussex TN31 7LB
Tele: 01797 229049
Website: ryetic@rother.gov.uk

Useful website links are given for each individual stage of the 1066 Country Walk, and also for all the circular walks in the second half of the book. Two very useful sites for tourist attractions etc are www.1066country.com and www.rother.gov.uk . Whilst www.wildhastings.org.uk is a very informative site on the nature reserves, and the many rare and protected species that live in the 1066 area. Finally I am indebted to Simon Mansfield, whose www.villagenet.co.uk site is a veritable mine of information on over 240 villages in the East Sussex and Kent area.

6. Public Transport

Basically the national rail service is reasonably good for getting you to the starting point at Pevensey Castle; the mid point at Battle; and at the finishing point in Rye. However in between you will have to rely on local buses if you want to vary/shorten your route, and please note that in many cases they either run infrequently or not at all on Sundays and bank Holidays!

Pevensey & Westham rail station is 10 mins walk from Pevensey Castle, the start of the 1066 Country Walk. This is between Eastbourne and Bexhill on the Southern Rail service from Brighton to Ashford International. It is also accessible from London Victoria via Lewes, and from London Charing Cross/Waterloo/London Bridge to Hastings, changing at St. Leonards Warrior Square. Once you've completed the 1066 Country Walk at Rye, then there is a regular rail service back to Hastings which takes 20 mins.

Check www.nationalrail.co.uk for journey planner details. Other useful sites, especially for bus timetables, are www.1066country.com and www.eastsussex.gov.uk .

The following buses run fairly regularly during the day from Monday to Saturday, but do check if travelling on Sundays and Bank Holidays:
- 98 bus from Bexhill to Eastbourne via Boreham Street. This is a useful link if you just want to do the first stage of the walk from Pevensey Castle to Boreham Street as a linear walk. That way you can catch the bus back to Bexhill station, and then get the rail connection to Pevensey & Westham.
- East Kent 100 bus runs from Hastings to Dover via Icklesham, Winchelsea and Rye. This is an extremely handy service if you simply want to do the final stage of the walk from Icklesham to Rye as a linear walk; the bus will have you back in Icklesham within 15 mins!
- 340/341/342 buses from Hastings to Northiam/Tenterden via Westfield. If you decide that you only want to go as far as Westfield, i.e. the end of Stage 4, then this service will take you back to Hastings rail station.

7. Accommodation

The author's website www.spanglefish.com/1066countrywalk has extensive information on the hotels, guesthouses, camping and caravan sites in the area. Simply click onto the ACCOMMODATION link. The main reason that these establishments are not listed in the book is that the website is much easier to update as businesses close down or start up; and the book would very quickly become out of date!

8. Pubs and Tea Rooms on the 1066 route
- PEVENSEY .... The Royal Oak & Castle Inn
- BOREHAM STREET .... The Bull's Head; Scolfe's Tea Rooms
- BROWNBREAD STREET, ASHBURNHAM .... The Ash Tree Inn
- CATSFIELD .... The White Hart
- BATTLE .... Martels (my personal recommendation!); A Taste of Battle; Pilgrims Rest; Jempsons; Ye Olde Kings Head; The Chequers
- WESTFIELD .... The Old Courthouse
- ICKLESHAM .... The Queen's Head (highly recommended!)
- WINCHELSEA .... The New Inn
- RYE ... The Mermaid; The George; The Ypres Castle; Jempsons; Haydens; Fletchers; Cobbles Tea Rooms

Poppies at Boreham Street

9. 1066 Feeder Links to Bexhill & Hastings

There are feeder links running off the 1066 route to both Bexhill (6 miles/10 kms) and Hastings (7.50 miles/12 kms). Both have white circular waymark discs on the signposts and stiles to distinguish them from the Country walk proper.

The 1066 Bexhill Walk starts at the halfway point of the entire route, just under ½ mile from Battle Abbey at the top of the hill leading down to Powdermill Wood. This goes through some very pretty countryside in Crowhurst and Combe Haven; the latter being a Site of Special Scientific Interest covering nearly 400 acres containing alluvial meadows and the largest reed bed in the county. It is a prime habitat for breeding birds and a wide variety of fauna; yet has the constant threat of the Bexhill to Hastings bypass hanging over it. The walk then continues on to finish in Bexhill Town Centre.

The 1066 Hastings Walk goes through even nicer countryside, starting at the footbridge over Doleham Ditch near Westfield and continuing on through Three Oaks, Guestling and up to North's Seat on the edge of Hastings Country Park. The park covering 660 acres is also an SSSI, containing sandstone cliffs, glens and many nature trails. North's Seat, at 575 feet above sea level, is the highest point in Hastings and on a clear day you can see the French coast with the naked eye! The walk then descends to East Hill, where it joins the Saxon Shore Way for a short distance to finish in Hastings Old Town by the seafront.

10. Long Distance Footpath links

The 1066 Country Walk essentially links the South Downs Way with the Saxon Shore Way at Rye. There are links from Pevensey to two points on the SDW national trail near to Jevington; the trail runs for 100 miles (160 kms) through England's newest national park from the white chalk cliffs of Beachy Head, near Eastbourne to the beautiful city of Winchester. The Saxon Shore way starts at Gravesend, Kent and traces the coast as it was in Roman times; this goes through Rye on its way to finish in Hastings. The 163 miles (262 kms) route was originally opened in 1980, and takes its name from the line of forts built by the Romans in the 3rd century as protection against the Saxon invaders from what is now southern Denmark. The route takes in the iconic white cliffs of Dover, the medieval port of Sandwich and Canterbury.

In addition there is a lesser known long distance path, the High Weald Landscape Trail, which runs for 90 miles (144 kms) from Rye to Horsham in West Sussex. This passes through the High Weald Area of Outstanding Natural Beauty (AONB), taking in such National Trust jewels as Nymans and Wakehurst Place, as well as the famous Bluebell Railway at Sheffield Park.

11. FAQs

- **How difficult is the 1066 Country Walk?** This is a pretty easy, generally low level walk with only tough climb at Tent Hill in Stage 3 (Ashburnham to Battle Abbey), and three lesser climbs in Stage 5 (Westfield to Icklesham). You can safely leave your oxygen cylinders, crampons and distress flares at home!
- **How busy can the walk get?** Although a popular walk with visitors, especially during the spring and summer, this is relatively quiet compared to walks in the Lake District. So walkers are definitely not going to be forming orderly queues behind one another!
- **Which is the most scenic stage?** Being a Westfield resident, I must admit to an element of bias, but for me it must be Stage 5 (Westfield to Icklesham). You have superb views heading out of Westfield towards Doleham, and then passing through Snaylham before dropping down into the Brede Valley.
- **Where are the most spectacular views?** Three views stand out for me, the most breathtaking being the view from the beacon at Winchelsea down into the Brede Valley in Stage 6 (Icklesham to Rye). Then there are superb panoramic views looking back from Steven's Crouch towards Ashburnham in Stage 3 (Ashburnham to Battle Abbey); and from the top of the track at Snaylham in Stage 5 (Westfield to Icklesham).
- **Other highlights on the 1066 route?** These are numerous and include Pevensey Castle; the Pevensey Levels; Herstmonceux Castle; Battle Abbey; Battle Great Wood, the glorious Brede Valley; the windmill at Icklesham, a well known local landmark with great panoramic views; the charming medieval town of Winchelsea; and finally Rye itself, a fascinating town crammed with hostelries, restaurants, tea rooms, art galleries and antique shops.
- **Is the route well marked?** Yes, the 1066 Country walk has both small marker posts and signposts all along the route, with red circular waymark discs on them and on the stiles. The Bexhill and Hastings links have white waymarkers to distinguish them from the main 1066 route.
- **Is it possible to do any of the 6 stages as a linear walk, and then use public transport to return to the starting point?** Yes, please refer to section 6 on Public Transport for more detailed information. However it is feasible to walk both Stage 1 (Pevensey Castle to Boreham Street) and Stage 6 (Icklesham to Rye) as linear walks, and return via public transport to the start.

12. 1066 Battle of Hastings – background

William Duke of Normandy sent up to 700 ships across the English Channel, landing his army at Pevensey on 28th September 1066. Meeting no resistance they camped overnight in the Roman fort at Anderida, and began planning their campaign to defeat King Harold of England. News of the invasion was soon carried to King Harold, who was forced to act with great urgency having only just defeated the Norwegian king Harold Hardrada at the Battle of Stamford Bridge (that's in East Yorkshire, and nothing to do with Chelsea FC!). He ordered his weary and depleted troops to march south, and by 6th October they had reached London having covered an astonishing 40 miles a day on foot. After a brief rest they continued south, and by the evening of 13th October the Saxons were assembled and camped at Caldbec Hill, some 6 miles from Hastings.

Battle commenced the following morning on 14th October with circa 7000 men on each side, and in the afternoon Harold was struck in the eye by an arrow and later cut down and killed by Norman knights. The high altar of the Abbey church was sited on the spot, but today a stone is all that is left of the place where the last Saxon King of England fell. The Norman victory allowed William of Normandy to take the English throne and become King. The battle sounded the death knell for the Anglo-Saxon way of life, and reshaped the destiny of this country by laying the foundations of the society, monarchy and nation that we know today. This was also the last successful invasion of England.

Battle Abbey was founded to commemorate the nearby Battle of Hastings, and is now famous worldwide. The original gatehouse is still intact, as are some parts of the Abbey, despite the dissolution of the monasteries during Henry VIII's reign. The town of Battle was gradually built around the Abbey, and later was a main producer of gunpowder until the time of the Crimean War.

13. The Countryside Code

Please respect the working life of the countryside, as our actions can affect people's livelihoods, our heritage, and the safety and welfare of animals and ourselves.
- Check the weather forecast before you leave, and don't be afraid to turn back if necessary.
- Follow the public footpaths wherever possible, particularly when crossing crop fields. Use gates, stiles or gaps in field boundaries when provided. Climbing over walls, hedges and fences can damage them, and increase the risk of farm animals escaping.
- Leave gates as you find them – a farmer will normally leave a gate closed to keep livestock in, but may leave it open so that they can reach food and water.

- Leave machinery and livestock alone, but alert the farmer if you think that an animal is in distress.
- Litter and leftover food not only spoils the beauty of the countryside, but can be dangerous to livestock and wildlife; so please take this home with you.
- Dog walkers – by law you must control your dog so that it doesn't scare or disturb farm animals and wildlife. On most areas of open country and common land, known as "access land", you must keep your dog on a short lead between 1st March and 31st July.... and all year round near farm animals. Not only are dogs liable to be shot by a farmer for sheep worrying, but the animals may end up losing their young owing to stress. Moreover a dog running amongst cattle is likely to be kicked or even trampled to death.

Inquisitive cows on the Pevensey Levels (Stage 1 Pevensey to Boreham Street).

Pett farmer Tim Jury is well placed to give advice, having farmed livestock for many years, and also being a fellow member of Hastings Runners! He says:" Your main concern should be for your own safety and those with you, so when passing through a field with animals such as horses and cattle take care not to scare them by walking/running through their midst. Better to deviate where necessary from the footpath and skirt round a herd or flock; walk/run slowly and steer clear of individual animals that have young, especially cows and their new born calves. It is very rare for animals to attack anyone, unless they are protecting their young!

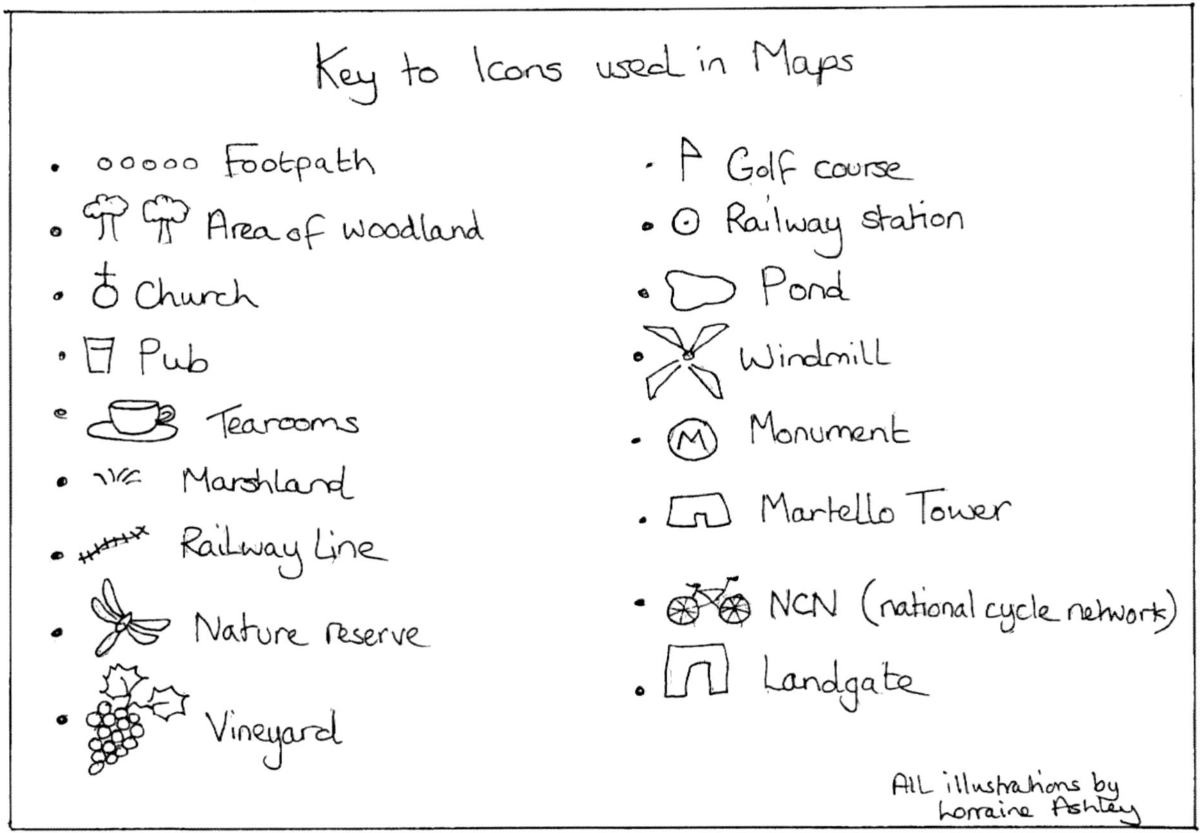

Key to Icons used in Maps

- ooooo Footpath
- 🌳 Area of woodland
- ☦ Church
- 🍺 Pub
- ☕ Tearooms
- ﹀⌣ Marshland
- ++++++ Railway Line
- 🦋 Nature Reserve
- 🍇 Vineyard

- ⛳ Golf course
- ⊙ Railway station
- ⬭ Pond
- ✺ Windmill
- Ⓜ Monument
- ⌂ Martello Tower
- 🚲 NCN (national cycle network)
- ⨅ Landgate

All illustrations by Lorraine Ashley

One of the author's favourite views at Guestling Thorn
(Circular Walk 4: Broad Street, Icklesham)

Pevensey Castle, the start of the 1066 Country Walk.

STAGE 1: PEVENSEY CASTLE TO BOREHAM STREET

The 1066 Country Walk begins beside historic Pevensey Castle, one of Britain's oldest fortresses; a truly inspiring way to commence your journey through the ages! For most of the first 5 miles you can enjoy the peaceful tranquillity of Pevensey Levels, a Site of Special Scientific Interest (SSSI) which was once completely underwater centuries ago, before reaching magnificent Herstmonceux Castle. A further 2 miles on through some more pretty countryside and you have reached Boreham Street, and the end of the first stage. Although the longest stage at nearly 7.50 miles, this is a very easy route apart from two steady climbs in the final 2 miles.

• 7.42 miles ascent 300 ft descent 198 ft RATING 2 ... EASY/MODERATE
• 93% off road paths; 1% off road hard track (rural); 4% quiet lanes; 2% main road (pavement)
• Suitable for walkers and dog walkers; you will generally find sheep in one field in section 4, and sometimes cows in the field in front of Herstmonceux Castle in section 5. However it is hard to predict the long stretches in sections 2 and 3

through the Pevensey Levels, as livestock are frequently moved!
- OS Explorer Map 124 Hastings & Bexhill
- Parking available for £2.00 all day in the Cattle Market car park next to Pevensey Castle. Public toilets next to the car park.
- Pevensey & Westham rail station on the Brighton/Eastbourne to Hastings line is just 10 minutes walk away
- Start ref: TQ 645047 Postcode: BN24 5LE
- Refreshments are available at The Bull's Head Inn and at Scolfe's Tea Rooms, both in Boreham Street. Please note however that currently the pub is closed on Monday lunchtime, and the tea rooms closed on Monday/Tuesday
- Websites: **www.english-heritage.org.uk**

THE WALK

Do take the chance to look round Pevensey Castle before starting your walk. It has been adapted to counter the threat of the Spanish Armada, Napoleon and Hitler during its long history, dating back to circa AD 300 when the Romans set up a fort named Anderida close to the sea at what is now known as Pevensey in East Sussex. The sea has since retreated some 4 miles away but the majority of the outer walls and the gateways are still intact, making it one of the longest surviving examples of a Roman fort in Britain. It assumed enormous historical importance when William the Conqueror landed in 1066, and remained in use until the 15th century when it was used as a prison. Since then it has been mainly unoccupied, except during times of war owing to its strategic defensive position. In 1925 the Duke of Devonshire gave the castle to the nation, and it is now one of English Heritage's most visited sites.

1. Starting beside **Pevensey Castle's East Gate**, take care crossing over the main road, **Castle Road**, to the pavement opposite as traffic visibility at this "S" bend is poor. Shortly after passing the **Priory Court Hotel** and **The Gables**, bear right at the 1066 Country Walk signpost onto an enclosed path which soon leads out into open countryside, rudely interrupted 300 yds later as you reach a bridleway gate next to the **A27**. Take great care crossing this main road, as the traffic is usually fast moving, to the bridleway gate opposite showing Rickney 2 miles.

2. Follow an enclosed path between fields, with a drainage channel **Martin's Ditch** on your left. This was probably excavated by a farmer of the same name when the harbour was drained more than 600 years ago. After 400 yds go through another bridleway gate, and you now follow a path across successive fields for the next 1 ¾ miles keeping **Pevensey Haven** on your immediate right, until reaching **Bridge**

Farm. (Ignore the footbridge on your right just under a mile into your walk leading into a conservation area). There you cross a stile to the left of the farm, and follow an enclosed path to a gate.

The Pevensey Levels.

3. Go through the gate and bear right onto **Rickney Road**, which soon leads to a T-junction. Turn right here onto **Rickney Lane** following the Pevensey and National Cycle Network route 2 signs, and you quickly cross a road bridge. Almost immediately turn left through a bridleway gate, where a 1066 signpost denotes Herstmonceux Castle 3 miles. Follow a path beside the river on your left for the next 2 miles; **the Yotham** which then becomes **Hurst's Haven** are upper reaches of **Pevensey Haven** which was Pevensey Harbour until the 13th century. Apparently birdwatchers have recently seen kingfishers here. After ¾ mile you start to go across a succession of fields linked by bridleway gates, still keeping the river on your left, You are eventually rewarded with a splendid panoramic view encompassing Windmill Hill windmill, All Saints Church and the large dome of the main telescope of the former Royal Greenwich Observatory, peering out above the treetops!

The **Pevensey Levels** are the largest tract of wetland in East Sussex covering 47 square miles, an important National Nature Reserve and an SSSI. The conservation area is owned jointly by Natural England with the Sussex Wildlife Trust, and is now recognised by ecologists as one of the finest in the world. There are many nationally rare plants, insects and invertebrates including the fen raft spider, aquatic molluscs and over 20 species of dragonflies. During the Roman period the shallow bay contained numerous small clay islands, which provided ideal dry sites for the first Roman settlements and were the origins of many modern day settlements such as Rickney – the suffix "eye" being Anglo Saxon for "island". These marshes started to be drained in the 13th century by a series of dykes, and gradually more of the wetland was reclaimed for agricultural use and the former bay ceased to exist. The following excerpt is from a Rudyard Kipling poem referring to the Pevensey Levels:

Trackway and Camp and City lost
Salt Marsh where now is corn
Old Wars, old Peace, old arts that cease
And so was England born

4. Eventually at the 4 ¼ mile point of the stage, a 1066 signpost directs you to bear right cutting off the corner of a field. Instead you follow a path across a scrubby field, usually with sheep in, with a hedge on your left until bearing left through a gateway. The observatory dome is looming ever larger! Cross the stile/gate and follow a path with ditches on either side until going through a bridleway gate into a large field. Now follow a wide grassy path which leads gently uphill across the field to a stile/gate at the far end. Then turn left onto a track, which continues uphill for 350 yds until reaching **Church Farm**. Bear right here and walk up through the centre of the farm for 150 yds until reaching a set of farm gates which are usually padlocked. Cross over these, and within 20 yds you have reached the bottom/dead end of **Church Road**. It would be criminal not to have a look round one of my favourite churches in the area, **All Saints Church**, which has great views across the marshes to the South Downs and whose entrance is just 50 yds further along on the left! Like many other churches in the area, the 12th century church is some way from the village, probably due to the Black Death in the mid 14th century when most villagers understandably distanced themselves from the churchyards where many plague victims were buried.

5. After your brief stop rejoin the 1066 Country Walk, and follow the path a short distance to a gate next to the driveway for **Church Farm House**. A 1066 signpost denotes Herstmonceux Castle entrance ¾ mile. Go through the gate and across some tarmac to a bridleway gate ahead. A woodland path then drops downhill to a gate from where you have a superb view of **Herstmonceux Castle** (see Circular

Walk 1 for photo). The castle is a magnificent building dating from 1441 with its towers and turrets reflected in the waters of its moats. Set in beautiful parkland and superb Elizabethan gardens, it was built originally as a country house and embodies the history of medieval England and the romance of renaissance Europe. The castle was home to the Royal Greenwich Observatory for many years, but the estate is now owned by the Queen's University of Kingston, Ontario, Canada who opened the Observatory Science Centre in 1995 and have been renovating the domes, buildings and telescopes. The grounds and gardens are open daily during the summer, but the castle isn't open to the public. Continue across the field and past an old, gnarled oak tree trunk, until reaching a bridleway gate. You have a great view of the main observatory dome from here!

Now follow an enclosed path as it climbs steadily uphill with the castle grounds on your left, until going past a disused car park and reaching **Wartling Road**. You have an excellent view at the top of the path across to your left of the remaining, resplendent green domes of the telescope buildings!

6. Turn right and continue along **Wartling Road** for 250 yds, taking great care as the traffic can be quite busy particularly at rush hours. Turn left onto a path just before reaching **The Well House**, and cross a stile leading into a field. Follow the path on the right hand side of the field, which leads across another stile into **Wartling Wood**. However after just 50 yds the path bears right out of the wood into a large field, where you then bear left and follow a path around the edge of the field until reaching a gateway emerging onto **Jenners Lane**.

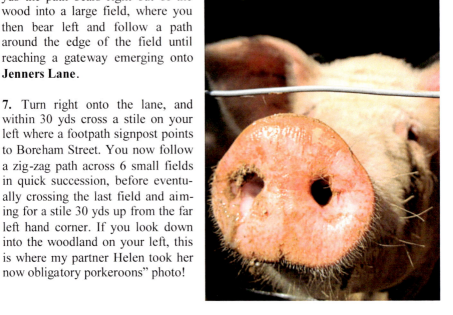

7. Turn right onto the lane, and within 30 yds cross a stile on your left where a footpath signpost points to Boreham Street. You now follow a zig-zag path across 6 small fields in quick succession, before eventually crossing the last field and aiming for a stile 30 yds up from the far left hand corner. If you look down into the woodland on your left, this is where my partner Helen took her now obligatory porkeroons" photo!

Go across the stile up ahead and continue ahead with woodland on your left. This field soon leads into another large field; follow the path ahead with a line of trees now on your right as it curves round at the top to the left. Just before reaching some barns at the end of the path, cross over the stile on the right and follow the enclosed path to another stile which drops down a stepped bank onto a narrow grass verge. You have great views from here towards Ashburnham.

8. Take care crossing over the traffic island on the **A271** main road to the pavement opposite. Then bear right and you will soon reach **Scolfe's Tea Rooms** on your left with **The Bull's Head** opposite. This is your only chance of refreshments before reaching the end of Stage 2 in 3 miles time!

All Saints Church, Herstmonceux

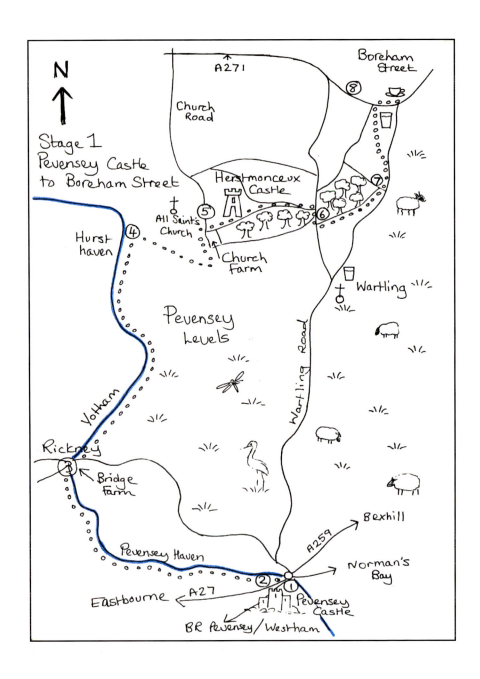

Great views towards Ashburnham as you approach Boreham Street.

STAGE 2: BOREHAM STREET TO ASHBURNHAM

The shortest of all the six stages at just under 3 miles, starting at The Bull's Head in Boreham Street and finishing at The Ash Tree Inn in Brownbread Street, which is part of the parish of Ashburnham... barely time to warrant slaking your thirst at the end of the stage! Some very pleasant countryside in between, but this gets progressively more spectacular in the latter stages of the 1066 Country Walk!

- 2.68 miles ascent 293 ft descent 251 ft RATING 1 .... EASY
- 20% off road paths; 5% off road hard track (rural); 65% private/unmade roads/ quiet lanes; 10% main road (pavement, some grass verge)
- Suitable for walkers and dog walkers; this is virtually a livestock-free route!
- OS Explorer Map 124 Hastings & Bexhill
- Car parking available in Wartling Village Hall car park, or in the lay-by next to this, on the A271 between Boreham Street and the Wartling Road turn-off to Herstmonceux Castle; also in The Bull's Head car park by arrangement.
- Start ref: TQ 666112 Postcode: BN27 4SG
- Refreshments are available at The Ash Tree Inn in Brownbread Street

• Websites: www.1066country.com

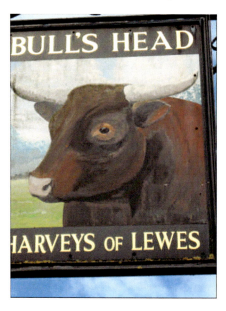

Boreham Street is part of the parish of Wartling, which in the Domesday survey of 1086 boasted a population of 280, woodland for 200 pigs, 3 salt workings and a chapel. Its name is probably derived either from the Anglo-Saxon "Beorgh Hamme" (village on the hill) or "Boar Hamme" (boar enclosure). In Roman times a road ran all the way from Lewes through here to Beauport Park in Hastings. The Bull's Head has been a coaching inn and then hostelry since the early 18th century, and comes complete with a resident ghost in its cellar!

THE WALK

1. Starting beside **The Bull's Head** in **Boreham Street**, turn right quickly passing **Boreham Lane** and **Harris Bros** garage on your right. Continue along the pavement for ¼ mile going past some delightful houses on either side of the main road, with splendid views on your left across the Ashbourne Valley. During the 17th century it would have been possible to see the smoke from Ashburnham Furnace, and the cannons being shipped downstream. Take care crossing over the **A271** at the brow of **Boreham Hill** to a 1066 signpost next to **Northfield House**, indicating Brownbread Street 2.50 miles. There is a 30mph speed limit sign next to the signpost.

2. Cross the stile, and follow the path across the centre of a paddock which usually has a couple of Shetland ponies grazing. Go through a gate, often left open, into a field and continue downhill to a gate hidden amidst the vegetation! Watch out for the huge rabbit holes halfway down on your right hand side! Go through the gate, and follow the path downhill to a stile next to a gate in the bottom right hand corner of the next field. Cross over this, then bear left and follow the path for a short distance to another stile/gate combination.

Cross over and continue straight ahead, keeping a ditch on your left. Bear left at the top of the field, before crossing over the footbridge on your right known as **Blackstock Bridge** which goes over the **Nunningham Stream**.

3. Bear left after crossing the footbridge, and soon the woodland path emerges into a large field. Follow the grassy path gradually uphill, with a fenced field on your left, until meeting a private drive leading to **Gardners Farm**. Continue straight ahead, ignoring the drive on your right, and follow the track to the left of the farm buildings which brings you out onto another track with a large field on your left. Continue climbing gently uphill, and after ½ mile you will pass **Wilson's Farm** on the right. Another 200 yds further and you have reached the end of the track at **Wilson's Cross**.

Fine views of Ashburnham from Wilson's Cross.

4. Turn right onto the lane (unmarked), and you have just over a mile to the end of the stage. First a steady descent down **Henley's Hill**, passing the Grade 2 listed **Henley Bridge Cottage** and then **Bray's Hill Farmhouse**, before a gradual climb up **Bray's Hill** to a T-junction. Continue straight ahead towards **Brownbread Street**, soon passing **Brownbread Street Horse Rescue centre** on your left. **The**

Ash Tree Inn is another 150 yds further along this narrow lane. You may well wish to refuel there, as the hardest stage of the 1066 Country Walk lies in wait!

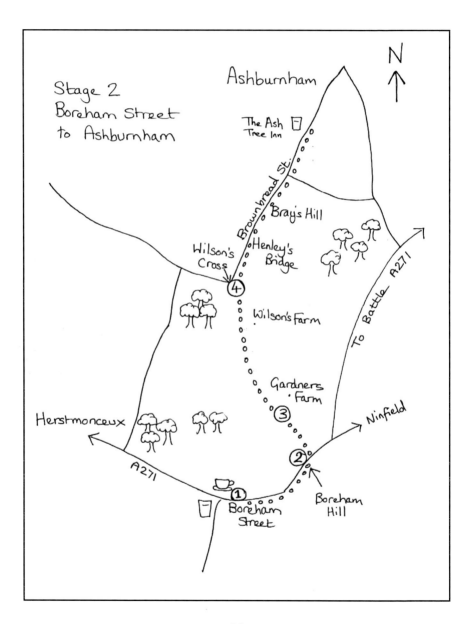

The panoramic view from Tent Hill.

STAGE 3: ASHBURNHAM TO BATTLE ABBEY

The second longest stage, and certainly the most testing with a severe climb up to the top of Tent Hill, where William the Conqueror's troops encamped on the eve of their historic battle with King Harold's army. The climb becomes more gradual as you continue up to Steven's Crouch, followed by a gentle descent on a public bridleway through the Normanhurst Estate all the way into the village of Catsfield. From there it is an easy 2 miles to the finish outside iconic Battle Abbey, apart from a tough climb on the final approach.

- 6.60 miles ascent 608 ft descent 528 ft RATING 4 .... TESTING
- 45% off road paths; 33% off road hard track (rural); 18% private road/quiet lanes; 4% main road (pavement)
- Suitable for walkers and dog walkers. Much of the route is livestock free, apart from sheep and sometimes cows in sections 3 and 4, and sometimes cows in section 9 approaching Battle Abbey
- OS Explorer Map 124 Hastings & Bexhill
- Travelling on the A271 from Battle, turn right ½ mile after passing the entrance to Ashburnham Place into an unnamed lane signposted Ashburnham Village and Heathfield. The lane drops downhill sharply, and after ½ mile turn left into another anonymous lane following the signs for Brownbread Street.

After ½ mile turn right at a junction following the Brownbread Street signs, and after 300 yds park in the lay-by on your right just before The Ash Tree Inn
• Start ref: TQ 676149 Postcode: TN33 9NX
• Refreshments available at The Ash Tree Inn at the start, The White Hart at Catsfield 2/3 rds the way round, or at Battle where I would highly recommend Martels in the High Street and in particular chef's bakewell tart – well more of a pie really, with lashings of black cherries; a meal in itself!
• Websites: www.1066country.com

THE WALK

1. **Brownbread Street** is a small community within the parish of **Ashburnham**, which derives its name from the Anglo-Saxon for "the settlement on the Ash stream". It is mentioned in the Domesday Book as having three salt houses, salt being a valuable commodity. It was also an important industrial area in the Weald district for many centuries thanks to its iron workings, and the Ashburnham blast furnace was the last in Sussex to be closed in 1813. Starting at the lay-by, go past **The Ash Tree Inn** and continue along the lane for 400 yds. Just after passing **Ashburnham Village Hall** on the left, go through a gate on the right where a 1066 Country Walk signpost directs you along the edge of two fields until reaching a gate at the far end.

2. Turn left onto the lane, and then immediately turn right onto another unnamed lane following the signs for Penhurst. The lane drops downhill quite sharply for the next ½ mile, passing **Old Forge Cottage** and the entrance to the **Ashburnham Estate**, both on your right. You will have fine views later on of **Ashburnham Place**, once one of the finest country houses in the South East in its heyday. The Ashburnham family controlled the village for an incredible 800 years!, until Lady Catherine the last in line died in 1953. Much of the house was demolished in 1959, having been badly damaged during the Second World War when a full loaded Marauder Bomber crashed nearby. Since being rebuilt it has been used for many years now as a Christian conference centre. The 250 acre park contains much ancient woodland, a medieval deer park and three large lakes designed by Capability Brown in the mid 18th century. Shortly after passing a track on your left leading to **Ashburnham Forge**, turn right by a footpath marker signposted **Steven's Crouch 1 ¾ miles**. Some fantastic views and hard climbing await you!

3. Follow a path across a small paddock, which then bears right beside a large garden which was once a nursery. Go through the gate at the end of the path, and head diagonally across a large field and then across the centre of the next two fields;

these are usually full of sheep. Cross the stile at the far end, and the path drops down to a footbridge over a stream. Then go directly across a narrow field to another footbridge, before scrambling up a bank at the edge of **Cowland Wood** leading to a stile at the top.

Tent Hill.

4. The steepest part of the stage now awaits you, **Tent Hill**, and thereafter you have a steady climb until reaching **Steven's Crouch**. Follow the steep path uphill, aiming just to the right of the small clump of trees in the photo above where the path thankfully levels off. Continue on until reaching a stile 50 yds to the right of a small fir tree plantation. You have great views across to **Ashburnham Place** on your right. **The next section is poorly signposted, so please pay particular attention!** Cross the stile, and head diagonally across the field to a copse on your left, where you will then find a footpath marker post just to the right of the copse but often obscured by vegetation. Continue in the same direction across the field passing another marker post, this time to the left of a copse, pointing towards a path going through a short stretch of woodland leading up to a stile. Go across this next field, passing a tree on your immediate right and a copse on your left. You will see a footpath marker by a water trough. Continue beside the copse for a short distance until reaching a telegraph pole. Now bear right and head diagonally uphill following the first line of pylons until reaching a stile in the top left hand corner of the field, with **Ashburnham Lodge** on your left. Cross the stile, and follow the path which soon emerges on the **A271**.

Inquisitive cows on the track leading down into Catsfield!

5. Take great care crossing over the busy main road to the track almost immediately opposite you, signposted **Catsfield 1 ½ miles**. After ¼ mile go across a stile on your left next to a gate, and then bear right following the track for nearly 1 ¼ miles all the way into Catsfield. This forms part of the 500 acre **Normanhurst Estate**, which dates back to the time of the Norman conquest. It is now a sporting and recreational estate within a working farm. You will often meet horse riders on this track as it is a public bridleway with a stables at the far end! After passing a small fishing lake known as **Horse Pond** on your left, go through a gate beside a cattle grid and **Wilton House stables** is on the right. The track now becomes a private road which within 150 yds brings you into the centre of **Catsfield**. Recorded as "Cedesfille" in the Domesday Book, the name was probably derived from the Anglo-Saxon Catt's Field (the field of Catt), or possibly from the Saxon tribe (the Catti) who settled there.

6. Turn left onto the pavement of the **B2204 Catsfield Road**, and **The White Hart pub** is immediately on your left and is your only chance of refuelling before the final push on to Battle! Continue along for 450 yds passing some delightful houses and cottages on your left, until going past **Parkgate Bungalows**. Turn left here and go diagonally right across the field to a stile next to gate, leading onto **Catsfield Road** again.

7. Take care crossing this often busy main road to the pavement opposite, and continue for 50 yds before turning right onto a track to **Starcroft Farm** with a 1066 signpost marker indicating **Battle 1 ¾ miles**. Cross the stile next to the gate at the end of the track, and continue across the field until bearing left over a gate into another field. Now follow a diagonal path which leads up through a field of Christmas trees to a stile in the top right hand corner. Cross the stile, and the path soon joins a main track in **Hoathybank Wood**. Go straight ahead for 100 yds before bearing left onto a path which drops steeply down a bank to meet a stile emerging onto **Farthings Lane**.

8. Turn right onto the lane, well more of a hard track really!, as it climbs gently uphill passing **Farthings Farm** on the left before descending to a gate at the bottom which marks the start of **Powdermill Wood**. Hard to imagine now, but for 200 years the powdermills in this immediate area made the finest gunpowder in Europe, supplying the British Army right up to the Crimean War. The works were closed in 1874 after a series of disastrous explosions. Go through the gate and the track now becomes a woodland path, where you may be lucky enough to spot some free range organic pigs rooting about in the woods on your right. Go through the gate at the end of the path, and the final climb of the stage awaits you. There are often cows in the next section.

9. Follow the path as it soon starts to climb steadily uphill with **Saxon Wood** on your left, until reaching a marker post at the top of the hill from where you have far reaching views. According to my Garmin Forerunner watch with its GPS navigation system, this is actually the true halfway point of the 1066 Country Walk, as you will have now covered just over 16 miles. Once you reach Battle Abbey you will have walked 16.70 miles with a mere 15.42 miles until the finishing point at Rye! Continue on to join a hard track, following this for 600 yds as it leads up to a gate with **George Meadow & Upper Stumblets** on the left. Go through the gate onto **Park Lane**, and **Battle Abbey** is just 100 yds further along.

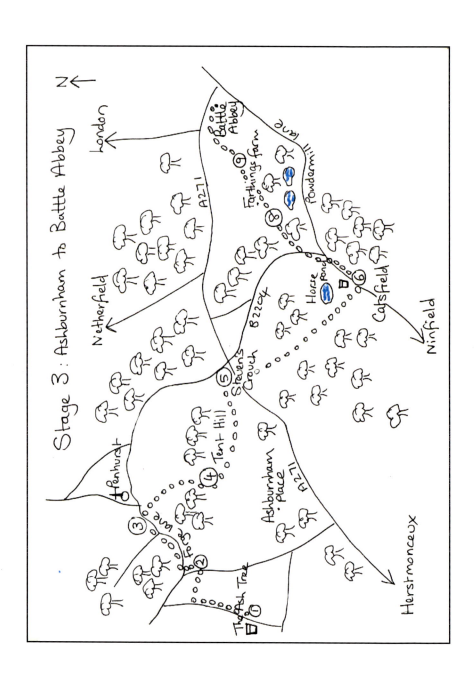

Battle Abbey.

STAGE 4: BATTLE ABBEY TO WESTFIELD

Starting the second half of the 1066 Country Walk, this is a very easy stage to get you underway with only a few minor climbs in Battle Great Wood to tackle as you head out towards the village of Westfield just under 5 miles away.

- 4.90 miles ascent 225 ft descent 374 ft RATING 2 ...EASY/MODERATE
- 63% off road paths; 8% off road hard track (rural); 10% private/unmade roads/ quiet lanes; 19% main road (mostly pavement, some grass verge)
- Suitable for walkers and dog walkers; there are sometimes sheep in several fields in section 5, and occasionally horses and cows in part of section 4
- OS Explorer Map 124 Hastings & Bexhill
- Parking available either in the Mount Street car park, just behind Battle High Street, or in the car park in Park Lane, 100 yds past the Abbey
- Battle rail station, on the London to Hastings line, is just 5 minutes walk away
- Start ref: TQ 749157 Postcode: TN33 0AD
- Refreshments – you are spoilt for choice in Battle – please see recommendations in Stage 3.

• Websites: www.1066country.com

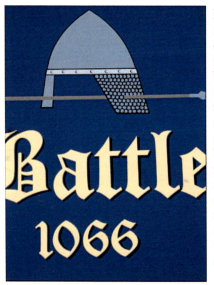

Battle Abbey is famous worldwide and was founded to commemorate the 1066 Battle of Hastings nearby. The original gatehouse is still intact, as are some parts of the Abbey despite the dissolution of the monasteries in Henry VIII's reign. You can walk round the original battlefield and actually stand on the spot where King Harold was slain. The town of Battle was gradually built around the Abbey, and later was a main producer of gunpowder. Most of the area was heavily wooded, and provided oak and other timbers for Navy shipyards, cannonballs and gunpowder. This small town is the heart of the Sussex Bonfires Society, which stages many celebrations during the autumn.

THE WALK

1. Starting outside historic **Battle Abbey**, walk down towards the Post Office with the **Abbey green** on your right. Once used for bear baiting, this area in front of the abbey gates is now used for more peaceful pursuits such as markets and entertainment. Cross over the zebra crossing in the **High Street**, and then turn right continuing along the pavement passing various shops including **Yesterday's World** which displays memorabilia from the 18th Century through to the 1970s. Shortly after passing **St. Mary the Virgin** church, founded in 1115 by Abbot Ralph, you come to a mini-roundabout. Bear left here passing **Lake Field**, acquired by the National Trust in 1938 to preserve the view to the north of Battle, and continue down **Marley Lane** for ¼ mile until reaching a **level crossing**. Continue over the level crossing for another ¼ mile, passing a residential estate on your left. The pavement peters out shortly after this, so cross over the lane to the pavement opposite. After passing **Harrier Lane** on your right, walk along the grass verge for another 200 yds passing **Blackfriars Oast** and **Greatwood Cottage** on your right.

2. You now come to a footpath signposted Westfield 4.5 miles ...don't worry it's actually only 4 miles! Turn right and follow the narrow path with a stream on your left leading you into **Battle Great Wood**, an area of 188 acres operated by The Forestry Commission. This consists of coniferous woodland, with areas of heathland, ponds, streams and sweet chestnut coppice, and is home to a wealth of wildlife including deer although these are generally only seen in the early morning or at dusk.

Battle Great Wood.

This narrow path soon becomes a much wider track, gently undulating, which you follow for the next ¾ mile going directly across three main track junctions. 100 yds after crossing the last junction, look out for the 1066 Country Walk signs on your right.

3. Turn right onto a much narrower path which heads quite steeply uphill at first before levelling off; this section can be quite boggy during the winter and greasy at any time of the year following rain. After 500 yds you emerge from the woodland onto **Sedlescombe Golf Course**; turn right and within 50 yds turn left onto a hard track which leads through the centre of the course...remember to look out for low flying golf balls! After 400 yds the track starts to bear round to the left; here you go straight across a fairway to a gate opposite. Follow a gentle downhill path for

150 yds to a large metal gate, which marks the halfway point of this stage. After passing **The Oasthouse** and **Norton's Farm** on your right continue for 400 yds down a private road until you reach the main road at **Kent Street**.

4. Bear left onto the grass verge, and shortly after crossing the entrance to **Sedlescombe Golf Club** cross over the **A21** to a gate opposite next to a house called **Buttonhole**. Take great care crossing this extremely busy trunk road. Go through the gate and follow an enclosed path between gardens until you reach a stile; cross this and follow the path across the centre of a large field to a gate leading into woodland. Much of this section between **Kent Street** and **Spray's Bridge** is invariably quite slippery following rain, and can be very boggy during the winter. After going through the gate, follow the woodland path as it crosses over a footbridge and leads to a gate further along the path. Now go across a farm track and, with a pond on your left, continue across a long, narrow field with fenced-in woodland (often containing free range pigs!) on your right and **Forge Stream** on your left. Cross a footbridge at the end of the field, then bear left before soon going through a gate leading into the field above. Bear right and follow the path through a gateway into the next field. Go across this field until reaching the raised walkway, and then follow a narrow path to a stile....watch out for the huge rabbit hole 50 yds after the walkway! Cross over the stile which brings you into a very rutted field where you will sometimes find several horses or sometimes cows. Bear left, and follow the rough track for 100 yds across a small bank to a stile which leads you onto **Wheel Lane**.

5. Take care crossing this deceptively busy lane, and walk downhill for 50 yds to **Spray's Bridge**. Just around the corner, on your right, is **Spraysbridge Farm**, a Grade 2 listed Wealden farmhouse built in 1691 which stands on the edge of an old Roman road leading from the site of iron ore workings on Platnix Farm to Sedlescombe. Cross over the footbridge on your left, and follow the path across a large field to a stile.

In the spring you may well hear the unmistakeable call of the marsh frog from the marshy area on the right! Cross the stile and follow the narrow path to a footbridge leading into a field. Go across the field to a footpath marker 80 yds ahead and slightly to your left; then across a raised walkway and up a woodland path leading to a stile. Cross the stile and follow the path which slopes gently downhill across a large field to a stream. Bear right at the bottom through a metal gate, and follow a narrow path leading to another gate. Follow the path beside the stream across the next three fields, all linked by gates, until reaching a footbridge on your left 100 yds into the last field.

Spraysbridge Farm

6. After crossing the footbridge you then have a sharp, but mercifully short climb along a track leading between paddocks to emerge on **New Cut**. This quiet lane has an interesting assortment of houses and bungalows, and probably existed around the time of the Napoleonic Wars. It is believed that some of the cottages were used by cavalrymen billeted in the village. Turn right, with **Horseman's Cottage** on your right, and follow the lane for 200 yds as it bears left going past **The Old Mission Hall** on your left. Then turn right onto an enclosed path dropping down to a footbridge over a stream, before heading uphill onto **Chapel Lane**. Follow this to its junction with **Cottage Lane**; you will see a Give Way sign and **The Old Stables** immediately ahead.

You have now reached my home village of **Westfield**! If you are stopping to refuel or for refreshments, then turn right onto **Cottage Lane** and then almost immediately right again onto the main road, the **A28**. A Londis grocery store is 100 yds along, and a further 100 yds along is The Old Courthouse pub, where you will get a friendly welcome and there's a garden area at the back.

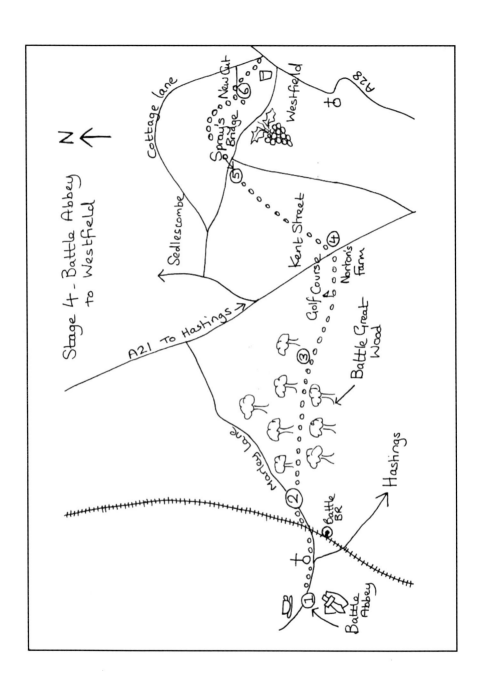

St. John The Baptist Church, Westfield.

STAGE 5: WESTFIELD TO ICKLESHAM

Being a Westfield resident I am obviously biased!, but having run and walked over the surrounding countryside for many years, I think that this next stage of just under 5 miles is the most scenic on the 1066 Country Walk. You have magnificent views heading out from Westfield towards Doleham, and then passing through Lower Snailham looking down into the Brede Valley before a steepling climb brings you into Icklesham. There one of the best pubs in the area awaits you with superb food and a panoramic vista!

- 4.90 miles ascent 469 ft descent 441 ft RATING 3 ... MODERATE
- 58% off road paths; 28% off road hard track (rural); 14% private/unmade roads/quiet lanes
- Suitable for walkers and dog walkers; there are often sheep present in many of the fields in sections 2, 4 and 6, and sometimes cows in part of section 5
- OS Explorer Map 124 Hastings & Bexhill
- No public car parks in the village; but there is plenty of residential parking
- Start ref: TQ 812157 Postcode: TN35 4QG
- Refreshments are available at The Old Courthouse, 2 mins walk away on the

junction of Wheel Lane and the A28
- Websites: www.1066country.com

Known as "Westewelle" in the Domesday Book; at this time there was a pit for "trial by water" in the village of **Westfield** which was owned by Robert, the Count of Eu who seemed to own virtually all the land between here and Herstmonceux! In 1291 the monks from Battle Abbey took over responsibility for the parish. Do take the chance to visit **St. John The Baptist Church**, which is just 5 minutes walk from the stage starting point. The pretty church dates back to the 12th century and is Norman in origin. Like many villages the church is some distance from the village centre because of the Black Death in 1348, and the number of plague victims buried in the churchyard. Westfield used to be a thriving commercial area with a forge and wheelwright, and indeed iron working played an important part in village life for many years.

THE WALK

1. Starting from the junction of **Chapel Lane** and **Cottage Lane, Westfield** turn left into Cottage Lane and within 30 yds take the path on the right beside **The Old Stables**. Take great care crossing the busy **A28** to a track opposite; you will see an interesting sign board commissioned for the Queen's Golden Jubilee in 2002 depicting the village's history. Continue down the track passing the doctor's surgery on your left, but as the track bears right follow a narrow path ahead through woodland (ignoring the track on your left!) leading onto the cricket pitch. Turn left and follow the path across the pitch to a gate. Go across a private road to a gate on your right. Follow the enclosed path to a stile which leads out into a large paddock where there are invariably horses in. They generally don't take much notice of people as this is a well trodden route. Go diagonally across the field to a gate in the far right hand corner, and follow a narrow path a short distance to the next gate. Now follow the path downhill with a crop field on your right which leads into another crop field; head diagonally across this field to a gate leading into yet another crop

field. The wood on your right goes by the most unusual name of **Pudding Cake Shaw!** Go across the centre of this field to a stile which leads onto a track.

2. Continue straight ahead and follow the track for 200 yds, passing **The First House** on your left and then **Pattletons Farm**, parts of which date back to the 14th century. Go over a stile on your left into a small paddock. As you start to cross the paddock which invariably has sheep in, you can admire the pretty oasthouse with its pond across to your right. Go over the stile at the end of the paddock, and then follow the path across the centre of a huge open field to another stile beside a copse with a pond. From here you have great views across to Doleham. The next two fields usually have sheep in. Now follow the downhill path to a footbridge over a stream called **Doleham Ditch**, which is a tributary of the River Brede.

Crossing the Doleham Ditch.

3. Cross the footbridge, ignoring the 1066 Hastings Walk sign to your right. You now face a sharp uphill climb, one of three on this stage with the hardest saved till last!, up into woodland before crossing the Ore to Ashford **railway line**. Take care getting over the two high stiles either side of the line, and obviously whilst crossing the track itself. Continue uphill across the centre of a scrubby field, bearing left at the top with a pond on your left and a house called **Ashenden** across on your right. Go through a gate at the end of the path which leads onto **14 Acre Lane**. Continue straight ahead, and within 200 yds passing the top of **Doleham Hill** with its line of pretty ex-railwaymen's cottages disappearing down into the valley. Follow the Guestling signs for another 600 yds, which gives you time to take in the superb views across to Westfield on your left. You will pass **Upper Lidham Hill** on your right and then **Lidham Hill Farm** on your left, before turning left onto a track leading to **Lower Lidham Hill Farm**.

4. Follow the track for 200 yds going through three gates, and then passing **Lidham Cottage** on the left as you follow a narrow enclosed path down to a metal gate at the bottom. Go through the gate and head diagonally across to a footbridge in the bottom right hand corner of the field. There are usually horses in both this field and the next one, but they generally ignore people. Crossing into the next field which sometimes contains some boggy sections, especially during winter, follow the path to a footbridge on your right. This marks the halfway point of this stage. Cross the footbridge and another one in quick succession, and then follow the path as it bears left skirting the edge of a large field, keeping the hedge on your right. Soon after crossing an earth bridge into the next field, bear right by a footpath signposted Rye and follow a meandering path across this scrubby field for 250 yds until reaching a stile on your left. Cross the stile and head uphill to another stile.

5. With **Lower Snailham Farm** on your left, you now face the second climb of the stage as the track heads sharply uphill for the next 600 yds. There are sometimes cows grazing in this area. The splendid views over towards Guestling on your right, and the Brede Valley on your left, are amongst my favourites in the 1066 area. The track thankfully levels off at the top as you reach a metal gate. The next wooded section of track is particularly lovely. Continue along the hard track ignoring a track on your left, and then passing a pond and **The Old Farmhouse** also on your left. Shortly after passing **Snaylham Farm**, you reach **Snaylham House**, which has stunning views over the surrounding countryside. Follow the track to a cattle grid at the end.

6. Turn left over the cattle grid onto a quiet lane **Broad Street**, and follow the signs for **Upper Brook House**. You pass through two gates next to cattle grids as the track zigzags down towards the valley going past **Brook Farm**. As the track peters out, then follow the path ahead to a gate at the bottom. Follow the path for 100 yds to a stile on the left. Cross the stile, then bear right following the path alongside a line of pylons to a footbridge at the far end of the field. You now face the steepest climb on this section, as the path goes up the centre of the field until

The wooded track at Snaylham.

reaching the top; then as it levels off start to bear left and aim for the stile in the top left hand corner.

7. Cross the stile and bear left onto a narrow path, which widens out to become **Parsonage Lane** within 200 yds. You will pass some houses on your right and a stable block with an outdoor school on your left. After another 150 yds turn left after **Parsonage Cottage**, and take a well earned break at **The Queen's Head**! The views from the garden over the Brede Valley are superb!

The steepling climb as you approach Icklesham.

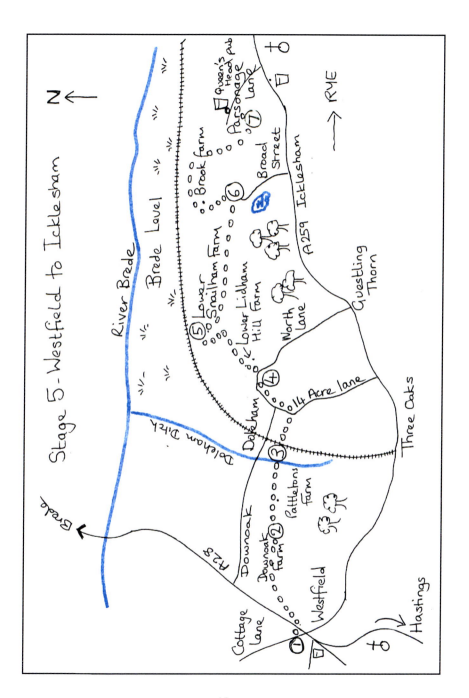

The windmill at Icklesham, a well known local landmark.

STAGE 6: ICKLESHAM TO RYE

The final stage of the 1066 Country Walk has some wonderful views over the Brede Valley and across to the English Channel, and has the bonus of being one of the easiest stages to boot! Were we across the Channel in Normandy, this stage would be called "La Route des Moulins a Vent", as it features the above windmill at Icklesham, another at the finish at Rye and at the halfway point in the delightful medieval town of Winchelsea stands a beacon looking out over the Brede Valley where once another windmill stood!

- 5.62 miles ascent 166 ft descent 304 ft RATING 2 ...EASY/MODERATE
- 40% off road paths; 22% off road hard track (rural); 36.50% private/unmade roads/quiet lanes; 1.50% main road (pavement)
- Suitable for walkers and dog walkers; there are usually sheep and sometimes cows present in many of the fields in sections 2,3 and 5
- OS Explorer Map 124 Hastings & Bexhill covers the whole route except for the last half mile; however this last section is so easy to follow that there is no need to buy the additional OS Explorer Map 125.
- Park in The Queens Head car park in Parsonage Lane, Icklesham, which is off the main A259 Hastings to Rye Road.

- Start ref: TQ 878165 Postcode: TN36 4BL
- Refreshments – you are spoilt for choice in Rye with a wide choice of pubs, restaurants, tea rooms and fish & chip shops. My gravitation towards tea rooms is legendary, but lately I have been straying to Jempsons in Cinque Ports Street, Rye, tempted by their delicious chocolate flapjack chased down with a frothy cappuccino at the bargain price of £3.00! There is also the friendly New Inn pub in Winchelsea, if you need to refuel just before halfway.
- Websites: www.visitrye.co.uk; www.winchelsea.net

THE WALK

1. Turn left out of The Queens Head pub car park into **Parsonage Lane**, and continue for 100 yds until reaching the **A259**. Take care crossing this busy main road into **Workhouse Lane** opposite. After passing **The Old School** and **Icklesham Village Hall** on your right, turn left immediately after **Chantry Lodge** where a 1066 signpost directs you onto an enclosed path. This leads past the churchyard of **All Saints & St. Nicholas Church**, with apple orchards on your right, onto a private drive passing **Stable Cottage, The Barn** and **Manor Farm Oast**. Follow the drive for a short distance straight ahead, ignoring another drive on your left, until turning left through a gate opposite a footpath signpost. This well marked path takes you through a number of apple orchards until you reach a gate in the hedge in the bottom right hand corner.

2. Turn left onto **Windmill Lane**, and within 50 yds cross over a stile on your left. Follow the path leading uphill towards the old post **windmill**, which has been restored and found a new use in the last 30 years, namely as a recording studio by Sir Paul McCartney! The panoramic views from the top of the hill are superb! At the foot of the hill cross over a stile onto **Wickham Rock Lane**. Turn left and continue for 150 yds. As the lane bears round to the left at **Hogs Hill**, cross over a stile immediately ahead next to a gate. Continue across the field, and cross over two stiles in quick succession leading into the next field. Continue straight ahead and enjoy the excellent views across to Pett Level on your right. Cross over a stile into another large field, following the path as it starts to bear left and heads downhill to a gate where you rejoin **Wickham Rock Lane**. There are invariably sheep grazing in these last two fields, and sometimes cows.

3. Turn right onto the lane, and within a few yards cross a stile on your left at the top of a small bank. Then follow the path downhill to a stile leading into another field; continue downhill aiming for a stile close to a telegraph pole, both of which are to the right of **Wickham Manor Farm**. Now owned by the National Trust, the

farm was once owned by William Penn, the founder of Pennsylvania. Cross over two stiles in quick succession, separated by a private drive, and go across the centre of a large field which often has livestock in. Across on your right is **New Gate**, one of Winchelsea's three surviving gates, built in circa 1330. Cross the stile/gate at the bottom, and continue across the centre of the next field for 150 yds until bearing right uphill to find a stile amidst the trees. Cross a narrow path to the stile opposite, which leads into a long narrow field where there used to be two hospitals many aeons ago. Bear left and head gradually uphill aiming for a rickety stile set into a wall, to the left of what used to be the **West Wall** of St. John's Hospital, an almshouse for the poor.

The West Wall at Winchelsea.

4. Go over the stile and cross the road (**Monks Walk**) to the pavement opposite, following the road as it bends round, keeping a wall on your immediate left. This leads into **German Street**, which takes you through the centre of the delightful medieval town of **Winchelsea**. Take time to look round the charming 13th century church of **St. Thomas the Martyr** and its lovely churchyard, and see the spot where John Wesley preached his last open-air sermon. As the road bears round to the right, continue straight ahead into **Hiham Green** before quickly turning left into **Mill Road** (neither residential road is actually marked!)

> **The Magnificent view from Winchelsea into the Brede valley – in my opinion the finest in the 1066 area!**

5. Take great care crossing over the **A259** to **Mill Lane** opposite, and follow this lane past the attractive **Mill Farm House** to a gate leading into a field. Shortly ahead of you is a bank which used to be the site of a windmill destroyed by the great storm on 1987. This was formerly the site of a Saxon church in the village of Iham ("high field") which disappeared at the end of the 16th century. Now just a beacon remains. The view from just in front of this spot, pictured above, is my favourite in the whole of 1066 Country! After admiring the view, go through the gate above and follow the path as it drops downhill, and curves round at the bottom to the right leading to a gate. Here, ignoring the footpath sign on your left, continue straight ahead with a line of tall trees on your immediate right. At the far end of the field cross over a footbridge on your right, and then follow the enclosed path which emerges at the foot of **Ferry Hill, Winchelsea**.

6. Turn left, and then immediately left again into **Station Road**. You now follow this meandering lane for nearly a mile, quickly passing **Ferry Bridge** across the **River Brede**. From here you have your first glimpse of **Camber Castle** across on your right. This was built in 1539 by Henry VIII to defeat the threat of French and Spanish invasion, but within 50 years the sea had receded thus rendering the castle obsolete. When passing **Newhouse pumping station** on your left, take the chance to admire the magnificent poppies in the field behind if you are doing this walk during June/July! After going over the **level crossing** at **Winchelsea Station**, the lane now becomes **Winchelsea Lane**, and continue until the junction with **Dumb Woman's Lane**.

7. Turn right onto Dumb Woman's Lane (origin unknown), and after 200 yds as the lane swings uphill continue ahead through a gate next to a cattle grid. For the next 1.25 miles you will be following the **National Cycle Network 2 route** along a hard track into Rye, with **Cadborough Cliff** – a haven for wildlife, especially birds – on your left. The cycle route currently stretches from Dover to Brighton, and is planned to reach St. Austell in Cornwall. After passing **Cadborough Waterworks**, the track soon leads onto the **B2089 Udimore Road**.

8. Turn right onto the pavement, and continue for 150 yds passing **Ashenden Road** until turning right into **Gibbets Marsh car park**. Follow the path on your left hand side which leads across the green to finish by the **National Cycle Network 2** sign opposite the **windmill**, a Grade 2 listed landmark, on the other side of the **River Tillingham**. Congratulations on competing the 1066 Country Walk, and enjoy a well deserved break in Rye!

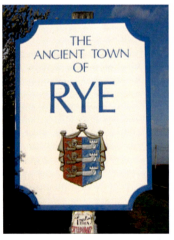

Rye has a well established reputation for its antique shops, art galleries, pubs and tea rooms! Its history can be traced back to the Norman conquest, and Rye was an important member of the Cinque Ports Confederation in medieval times. It was better known for its smuggling activities during the 18th and 19th centuries; wool and luxury goods being the largest commodities. Famous people who lived in Rye include Spike Milligan and numerous authors including Henry James, Rumer Godden and Russell Thorndike who set his Dr. Syn about smuggling on the nearby Romney Marshes.

The Gun Garden, looking across Rye Harbour.

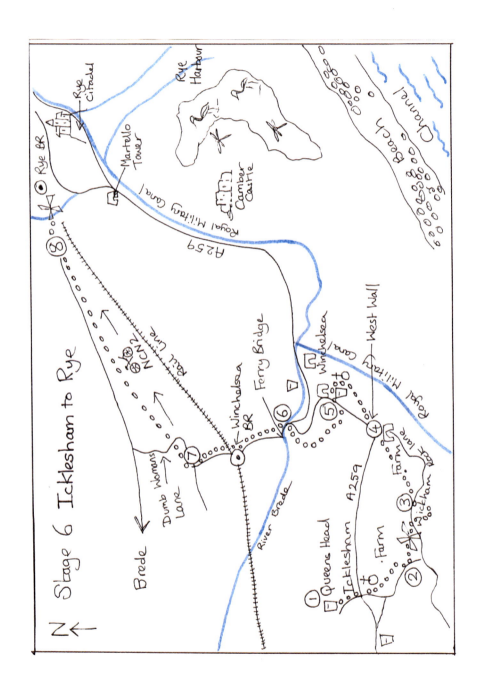

The finish of the walk in Gibbets Marsh car park.

Herstmonceux Castle.

CIRCULAR WALK 1: HERSTMONCEUX

A very enjoyable route of nearly 6 miles with stunning views of Herstmonceux Castle, Herstmonceux Place, Windmill Hill Mill and surrounding countryside including the South Downs. The opening ¾ mile as you go downhill past the castle to All Saints Church along the 1066 Country Walk path is one of my favourite starts to any route.

- 5.80 miles ascent 460 ft descent 465 ft RATING 3 …. MODERATE
- 63% off road paths; 3% off road hard track (rural) 28% quiet lanes; 6% main road (pavement)
- Suitable for walkers and dog walkers: there are usually sheep and sometimes cows in sections 1,2, 3, 5 and 7
- OS Explorer Map 124 Hastings & Bexhill
- Park in the lay-by on Wartling Road, just to the right of the main castle entrance. Wartling Road runs off the A271 from Battle to Herstmonceux
- Start ref: TQ 653103 Postcode: BN27 1RN
- There are no refreshments en route, but on finishing I would recommend adjourning to The Lamb Inn, a delightful 16th century pub in nearby Wartling
- Websites: www.herstmonceux-castle.com

THE WALK

1. Starting at the lay-by, go past the entrance to **Herstmonceux Castle** and turn right at the 1066 Country Walk sign for Pevensey. This takes you quickly past a disused car park and into woodland. Follow the path across a private track and then through a gate as it drops downhill to give you a superb view of the castle on your right. Go through the gate at the bottom into an open field with an impressive gnarled oak tree trunk just to your left. Head across the field to the gate opposite, and then follow a short uphill path to the next gate. Continue across the drive to another gate which brings you out onto **Church Road**. Here we leave the 1066 Country Walk, but will rejoin it later for the final ¾ mile.

Windmill Hill windmill.

2. Bear right and pass **All Saints Church** on your left. This superb church dates back to the 12th century, and has commanding views over the Pevensey marshes towards the South Downs. Continue along the lane for 200 yds before taking a path on your right through woodland. You will soon pass a crossroads footpath signpost, but continue straight ahead until reaching a gate at the end of the path. You have magnificent views ahead of you with **Herstmonceux Place** over to your left; this impressive looking building was built with bricks from the nearby castle in the late 18th century, and has a fine classical facade. Follow the path downhill past a water trough and some trees.

Great views heading towards Comphurst Lane

A short but steepish climb now awaits, keeping the fence to your left. At the top of the hill go through the gate ahead, and onto a narrow path which goes through a copse before widening into a track.

3. Follow the track as it climbs gently uphill, passing a house on your left as the track now becomes **Comphurst Lane**. You will soon reach a stile on the left where you have your first glimpse of **Windmill Hill Mill** up ahead; take time however to admire the house opposite, **Comphurst**, and its superb Norman-style front door. The windmill is the largest post mill in Sussex. Built in 1814 and worked until 1893, it has recently been restored and is now computer controlled with an automatic turning device which relies on wind direction sensors ... all clever stuff! Proceed across the field which sometimes contains horses to a stile, which drops down steeply into the next field. This field often has cows in. Follow a diagonal path downhill, and then leading up to a stile to the right of **Allfree Wood**. Cross over the stile and follow the path as it winds its way round the side of the wood to emerge on the **A271**.

4. Turn left and continue along the main road which thankfully has a wide pavement for 500 yds, before turning left into a quiet lane **Chapel Row**. After 300 yds you pass a former pub **The Welcome Stranger** and then **Herstmonceux Free Church** on your left. Bear right opposite the church and the path leads you into **Lime Park**.

5. After going through the gate into **Lime Park**, bear left and follow a well trodden path slightly uphill with houses on your left to a gate. This is a short cut from the official footpath, but as it's in a park you needn't worry! After going through the gate and across a short section of tarmac, continue across the centre of the field which is divided by a track and two small gates, dropping downhill to a stile at the bottom. Cross this and continue downhill to another stile. This brings you onto a track where you turn right, with a pond on your right, and then within 50 yds bear left beside another pond into a large open field. Go across the centre of this field to a copse, and follow the path down to a footbridge leading into the next field. Continue across the field to a stile which emerges on **Lower Road**, with a minor road opposite you.

6. Turn left onto **Lower Road** and continue along this quiet lane for ¾ mile passing several farms on your right and **Butler's Lane** on your left. Bear right at the junction with **Church Road**, just after passing **Cherry Croft Farm** and its pond on your right. After ¼ mile the lane starts to steepen, and you have a testing climb up towards the church. Bear left at the end of the lane, and go through a gate on your left just before the entrance to **Church Farm**.

7. You now rejoin the 1066 Country Walk and follow your outward route for ¾ mile back to the start.

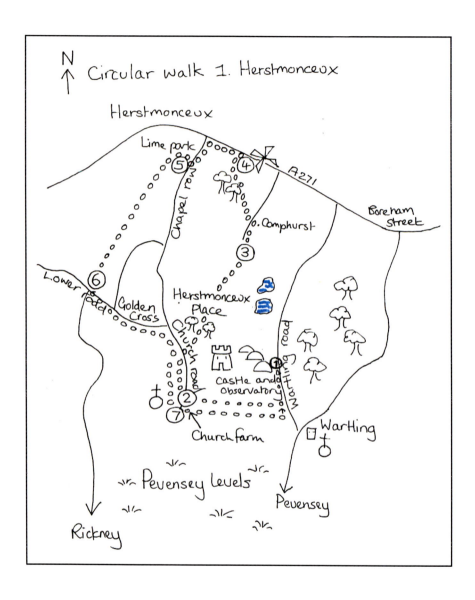

Battle Abbey.

CIRCULAR WALK 2: BATTLE

A very scenic route of just under 6 miles starting and finishing outside historic Battle Abbey, with some delightful views as you head outwards Catsfield on the 1066 Country Walk path. Passing close to Powdermill Wood where the finest gunpowder in Europe was said to be made, you may glimpse the free range organic pigs featured in my previous book Walks in 1066 Country!

- 5.70 miles ascent 691ft descent 729 ft RATING 2.... EASY/MODERATE
- 53% off road paths; 24% off road hard track (rural); 21% private/unmade roads/quiet lanes; 2% main road (pavement)
- Suitable for walkers and dog walkers; there are sometimes cows and sheep present in sections 1, 7 and 8
- OS Explorer Map 124 Hastings & Bexhill
- Parking available – cheapest either in the Mount Street car park, just behind Battle High Street, or at Budgens/Jempsons at the top end of the High Street
- Battle rail station, on the London to Hastings line, is 5 minutes walk away
- Start ref: TQ 749157 Postcode: TN33 0AD
- Refreshments – I highly recommend Martels in the High Street!
- Websites: www.1066country.com

THE WALK

1. Starting outside **Battle Abbey**, continue along **Park Lane** past the car park onto a hard track which leads to a gate opening into **George Meadow & Upper Stumblets**. This is pretty well the halfway point of the 1066 Country Walk. Go through the gate and continue along a track with woodland on your left for 600 yds until reaching a marker post at the top of the hill which gives you wonderful countryside views. Bear right here following the Pevensey signs, and you can enjoy a lovely downhill section to a gate in the bottom right hand corner of this field. Please note that there are sometimes cows grazing both along the track and in this field.

The view towards Powdermill Wood.

2. Go through the gate and follow the woodland path to the next gate. You may be lucky enough to spot some free range organic pigs rooting about in the woods to your left! In 1676 John Hammond was licensed to build a powdermill on land owned by Battle Abbey. Other mills then sprang up in the area, and were said to make the finest gunpowder in Europe supplying the British Army right up to the Crimean War. The works were closed in 1874 after a series of disastrous explosions. Nearby **Powder Mills Hotel** is built on the site of the gunpowder works. Go through the gate at the end of the path, and continue along the track as it climbs gently uphill passing **Farthings Farm** on the right. The track then descends, and after 300 yds cross a stile on your left. This takes you into **Hoathybank Wood**, where the path climbs steeply up the bank ahead of you before levelling off just before meeting a track junction. Turn right and as the track starts to swing left, bear right onto a narrow path which soon leads to a stile. Cross over and head diagonally downhill across a field of Christmas trees to a gate at the bottom. Go through the gate and then bear right, following the path to a stile/gate. Then follow a hard track which leads you out onto the main **Catsfield Road**.

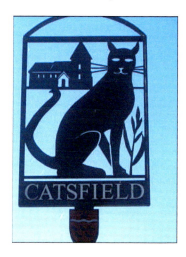

Recorded as "Cedesfille" in the Domesday Book, the name **Catsfield** was probably derived from the Anglo-Saxon Catt's Field (the field of Catt), or possibly from the Saxon tribe (the Catti) who settled here. In 1791 Princess Lamballe, one of Marie Antoinette's ladies in waiting, was sent with the queen's jewels for safe keeping to Lady Gibbs at **Catsfield Place**, which you will see as you drop down towards **Catsfield Place Farm**. For those wanting refreshments at this early stage, follow the main road for ¼ mile into **Catsfield** until reaching The White Hart pub.

3. At this juncture we leave the 1066 Country Walk, but will rejoin it for the final ½ mile of the route. Turn left onto the pavement and continue for 200 yds until reaching the junction with **Powdermill Lane**. Cross straight over the lane, taking great care, into the driveway of the house opposite, **Horn's Hill**. Go through the gate immediately ahead of you and follow the path, which is clearly marked, across the next three fields. You will pass a tennis court on your right, and occasionally meet llamas in the last field! On going through a gate into the next field, follow the path diagonally downhill to a gate emerging on **Church Road** opposite **Catsfield Primary School**.

4. Turn left and continue along the pavement which soon leads you up through the churchyard of **St. Laurence Church**. The church which dates mainly from the 13th century is shaded by a mighty oak, one of the oldest in Sussex. Two of its bells are amongst the oldest in the country, being cast in 1408 and 1418. The famous engineer **Thomas Brassey** is buried in the churchyard. He built Britain's

Great Northern Railway, Canada's Great Trunk Railway as well as railways across the Alps, Argentina, India and Australia. Continue along the lane passing **The Rectory** on your left, before going up a short hill passing **Potman's Lane** on the right. Turn left soon after the top of the hill into a driveway leading to **Church Farm**, but almost immediately cross the stile on your right into a field.

My partner Helen striding out of St. Laurence churchyard!

5. Follow the path to a gate to the right of the farmhouse, and then go through two small paddocks into a larger field containing horses. You have great views towards Battle across to your left. Cross this field to a stile in the centre, and them aim for a stile just to the right of a copse in the top left hand corner of the next field. The next part of the route is poorly marked, but basically you are aiming for the centre of **Catsfield Place Farm** which you will see down below. Beyond that you have a splendid view of **Catsfield Place** which is now a school. Once you've crossed the stile turn left and head downhill to the bottom of the field; then bear right and continue along the edge of the field until you are about halfway across. Now take the path on your left running parallel to the field, leading up between farm buildings at **Catsfield Place Farm**. Go up the farm drive; then turn left onto a hard track which drops downhill.

6. Follow the track round to the left, and you then have to skirt round a boggy piece of ground which is at a junction of footpaths. Continue straight ahead into a field, and head uphill until you reach the top where you will see a metal gate across to your left. Go through this and you are at the far end of **Peppering Eye**, a private road which you follow for over 1.25 miles until reaching **Telham Lane**. You will pass a number of cottages as well as **Peppering Eye Farm** and **Old Peppering Eye Farmhouse**.

7. After going through the gate near the end of the lane, turn left into **Telham Lane**. Within 100 yds you reach the busy junction with **Powdermill Lane**; take great care as you cross the road to a steep bank with a stile at the top. Follow the path which climbs gradually uphill, and runs parallel to the lane; **Powdermill House** is over to your left. Go over the stile at the top, and cross the private road to the stile opposite. This leads onto a hard track which drops downhill, with a fenced-in field on your left, until reaching a softer track heading uphill through two gates. You then face a steep climb aiming for the solitary tree at the top of the hill, but the path keeps on climbing for another 100 yds until levelling off just before

A steep climb to rejoin the track leading back to the Abbey!

the footpath marker that you passed in section 1.

8. Bear right after the marker, where you rejoin the 1066 Country Walk, and follow your original path for ½ mile back to the **Abbey**.

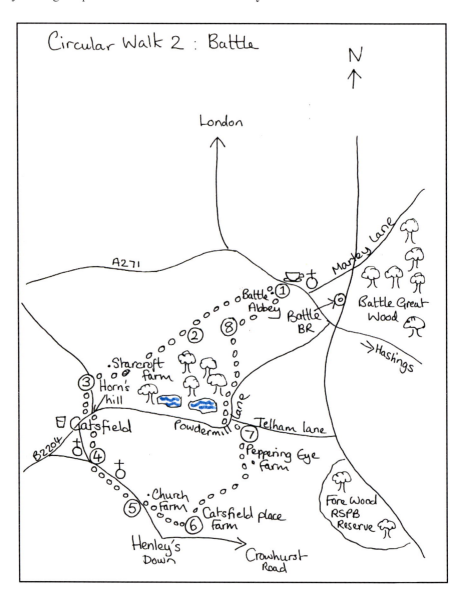

My partner Helen by the halfway point of the 1066 Country Walk, just before reaching Battle.

Great Maxfield.

CIRCULAR WALK 3: WESTFIELD

An extremely enjoyable route of nearly 5 miles with some lovely views of the surrounding area, taking in the hamlet of Great Maxfield and Pattleton's Farm which is thought to be the oldest house in the area. Most of the route back from Doleham into Westfield follows the 1066 Country Walk path.

- 4.90 miles ascent 525 ft descent 656 ft RATING 3 .... MODERATE
- 75% off road paths; 6% off road hard track (rural); 16% quiet lanes; 3% main road (pavement)
- Suitable for walkers and dog walkers; there are sometimes sheep in sections 4,5 and 7, but otherwise this is a relatively livestock free route!
- OS Explorer Map 124 Hastings & Bexhill
- Park by the side of the road (The Moor) opposite The Plough, or indeed in the pub car park if you are planning to visit there afterwards! Westfield is on the A28 Hastings to Ashford road; turn right as you enter the village at the first main junction opposite The Old Courthouse into Moor Lane, and The Plough is ½ mile further along.
- Start ref: TQ 814151 Postcode: TN35 4QR
- Refreshments are available at The Plough which has a garden area
- Websites: www.1066country.com

THE WALK

1. Starting at **The Plough** cross over into the track opposite, which has a stone footpath marker on the right, and continue to a gate at the end of a track which leads into a large field. Follow the path across the centre of the field to a footbridge which takes you into a vast field; this used to consist of a collection of really lovely fields divided up centuries old hedgerows . Unfortunately some years ago the landowner ploughed up the entire area, including hedgerows, and thus sadly changed the nature of this landscape for ever. So head uphill and slightly to the right until meeting a path at the top of the hill. Bear left onto the path and continue along with a pylon on your right. Just after passing a copse on your right, the path bears right and heads diagonally down to a footbridge at the bottom left hand corner of the field. **Oak Wood** is over on your left hand side.

2. Cross the footbridge and continue across a narrow field to a stile. This section is often extremely boggy in the winter! **Please note that the next part of the route to Great Maxfield is very poorly signposted, so please follow the directions carefully!** Cross the stile and follow the path through a short section of woodland leading into a large field. Then head uphill keeping a hedge on your left. At the top you will see a small gap in the undergrowth (no markings!), and a path through the copse leads you onto a track. Turn right along the track, and after 50 yds turn left to follow a rough path along the edge of a field heading downhill. Turn right at the bottom and cross a private road to a stile opposite.

3. As you cross the stile you will see a large man-made lake in front of you. Bear left, and you will soon be greeted by another lake with a splendid view of the back of **Great Maxfield House**, an old timbered building believed to date back to the 15th century. Follow the path uphill to a stile next to a gate with the warning "bull in field" … don't be too alarmed as I have never seen this creature in 20 years of running this route! However do pay great attention to the deep rabbit holes which litter this field! Continue to the top of the hill, bearing left at the footpath marker and follow the path until you come to a gate ahead of you. Turn right instead over a stile, where we now join the 1066 Country Walk feeder link to Hastings for a short section, and cross over a railway bridge spanning the Ore to Ashford line. Cross over another stile which takes you into a field. Follow the path across the centre of the next three fields, but halfway into the fourth field bear left as the path forks and aim for a gap in the top left hand corner of the field. Upon going through this gap into the next field, continue bearing round to the left and follow the path to a stile in the corner. Cross the stile and follow the path, which is bordered by trees on the left and by a huge garden on the right, until you reach a stile at the end of the path. Cross this and go straight across the field to a gate which emerges onto **14 Acre**

Lane.

4. Turn left onto the lane and continue for a kilometre passing some pretty cottages further along. As the lane begins to swing right, bear left over a gate next to a house called **Ashenden** where a marker post indicates that we will be following the 1066 Country Walk for most of the way into Westfield. Follow the path as it bears right with a pond over to your right, and heads sharply downhill to cross the same railway line you crossed earlier in section 3. Take care getting over the two high stiles either side of the line, and obviously whilst crossing the track itself. You are then in an open field with great views of Westfield and Doleham, as you head downhill to a footbridge over the **Doleham Ditch**.

Superb views from Doleham towards Westfield.

5. After crossing the footbridge, you now have a punishing climb towards the copse at the top of the hill opposite! As you cross the stile to the left of the copse, you can enjoy a well-earned breather looking at the excellent views of the countryside. Then follow the path across a large field to a stile which leads you into a small paddock, invariably containing sheep. There is a tennis court over to your left. Cross the paddock to a stile in the far right hand corner which brings you out onto a track. Turn right and you will immediately see **Pattleton's Farm**, parts of which date back to the 14th century. Follow the track for 250 yds passing a house called **The First House** on your right. Just before the track starts to swing round to the right, go over a stile immediately ahead.

6. Follow the path across the centre of the field to a gate; the wood on your left goes by the most unusual name of **Pudding Cake Shaw!** After going through a gate into the next field, follow the path diagonally across to a gap in the bottom right hand corner leading into another field. Then follow the grassy path uphill, but just before reaching the top of the hill go through a gate on your right hand side. Follow this enclosed path which borders a garden to the next gate, which leads into a large paddock usually containing horses. Go across the paddock, often divided into two, aiming for a stile next to a telegraph pole in the far right corner. Cross the stile and a short section of path leads you to a gate bringing you out onto a private road.

7. Cross the road to a gate opposite for **Westfield Cricket Club**. Then follow the enclosed path, with woodland to your left and a field on your right, until meeting an unmade road. Here we leave the 1066 Country Walk and cross over this to join a path with a house initially on your left, before the path bears right through woodland to a gate at the far end. Go through the gate into a field, and continue ahead to another gate; go through this into a narrow field and within 100 yds cross a stile on your left. Turn right onto what is the end of **Fishponds Lane** and follow this rough track until its junction with **Workhouse Lane**. Turn left at the end onto **Moor Lane**, and continue along the pavement for 300 yds back to the start.

Looking back towards Doleham

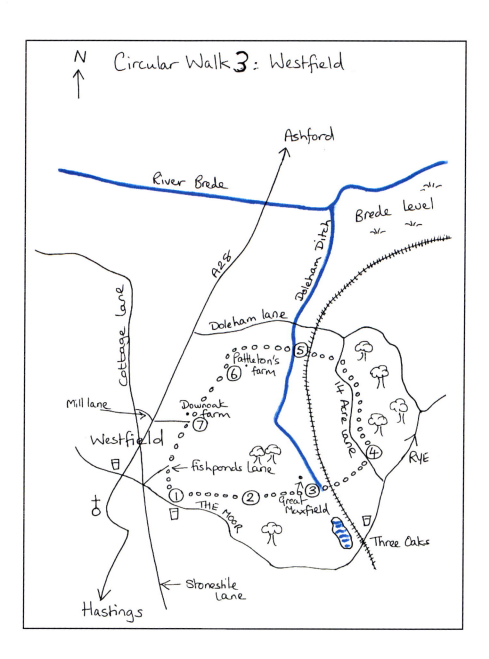

Broad Street fishing lake, Icklesham.

CIRCULAR WALK 4: BROAD STREET, ICKLESHAM

A very pleasant 4.50 mile route following the 1066 Country Walk path for most of the opening mile, with some glorious views heading down towards Lower Snailham. The middle section has great views of Guestling towards Pett, before crossing back over the A259 and dropping down sharply into the Brede Valley where you rejoin the 1066 path for most of the final section.

- 4.50 miles ascent 444 ft descent 442 ft RATING 2 .... EASY/MODERATE
- 50% off road paths; 24% off road hard track (rural); 22% private/unmade roads/quiet lanes; 4% main road (pavement)
- Suitable for walkers and dog walkers; there are invariably sheep in sections 2, 6 and 7, and sometimes cows around Lower Snailham Farm in section 1
- OS Explorer Map 124 Hastings & Bexhill
- Park in the Broad Street fishery lake lay-by 600 yds along Broad Street, a left turning off the A259 Hastings to Rye Road, just before reaching Icklesham
- Start ref: TQ 864165 Postcode: TN36 4AS
- There are no refreshments available en route, but afterwards you can retire to either The Robin Hood Inn or The Queen's Head, both in nearby Icklesham
- Websites: www.1066country.com

THE WALK

1. Turn left out of the car park into **Broad Street**, immediately passing two quaint holiday cottages on either side, namely **The Stable** and **Garden Cottage**. 300 yds further along the lane, after passing another two picturesque cottages on your left, bear left over a cattle grid where you will join the 1066 Country Walk path. Follow the hard track past the impressive **Snaylham House, Snaylham Farm** and **The Old Farmhouse**, with great views across to the Brede Valley on your right. You then have a lovely wooded section of track leading to a farm gate; dropping downhill to **Lower Snailham Farm** you are rewarded with further splendid views, this time across to Guestling on your left and Doleham straight ahead.

The track leading down to Lower Snailham.

2. At the bottom of the track turn left – **Lower Snailham Farm** is on your right – and follow a track leading gently downhill to a gate. Go across the field to another gate, where you now face a steady climb uphill. Go through a gateway into the next field, continuing past a cattle grid with a pond on your left, aiming for some farm buildings at the top of the field. Continue on past the buildings to a track at the very top, where there is a junction of footpaths. Go through the gate onto a track, passing **Stocks Farm** on your left. Soon the track converges; bear right past the pond and tackle a short but demanding climb. At the top you join the entrance to **Harborough Nurseries** at **Guestling Thorn**.

3. Take great care crossing over the busy **A259** to the grass verge opposite, continuing on for 80 yds until reaching a stile beside a gate. Go across the stile and follow the path across the centre of a cornfield. From here you can see Pett Church and Fairlight Church in the distance ahead. Go down a bank at the end of a field, next to a stile hidden in the undergrowth, and then across the centre of the next field where the path is usually non-existent! As the field narrows, you will see a marker. Continue ahead with the line of fencing on your left before heading diagonally across past a pylon to the right of a copse. Go through a metal gate and then through a gap in the hedge opposite, following a woodland path snaking downhill to a gate leading onto **Watermill Lane**. You have just passed the halfway point of the route.

4. Turn left onto **Watermill Lane**, which is quiet and very narrow. After 500 yds you will pass **Old Oast Place** on your left, and almost immediately go through a very well secreted gap in the hedge on the left to cross a stile. Then follow an enclosed path with a hedge on your left and a field on your right, as it leads gently uphill. Follow the path as it winds its way round into the next field, continuing uphill until reaching a footbridge on your right leading into a copse. The path goes up a steep bank, at the top of which you are suddenly confronted by a wooden fence. Continue ahead keeping the fence on your right, before crossing over a private drive to the path opposite. After doing a limbo impression to get under the very low overhanging branch!, follow the path across a field which is often overgrown for the first 50 yds until reaching a gap in the hedge next to a gate. The stile is buried in the vegetation! This brings you out opposite **Broad Street**, just 600 yds from where you started.

5. Take care re-crossing the **A259** to the pavement opposite, then bear right and continue along the pavement for 350 yds. Turn left after passing **The Firs** into the driveway for **Toke Farm**. Go through the gate to the left of the entrance, and continue along the driveway for 80 yds. Bear left just before reaching the farmhouse onto a narrow enclosed path leading to a stile. Cross the stile, then duck under another low branch and the path leads you into a large field. **The footpath signs aren't very clear for this next section, so please pay particular attention to the directions!**

6. You will see a footpath marker straight ahead. Go downhill on the left hand side of the field to a stile. Cross the stile, then bear right through a gateway into another field. Having gone through the gateway bear left following an indistinct path. Basically try to keep to the left hand edge of the field, going through a gap in the edge ahead leading into another large field. From here you have great views across the Brede Valley. Keeping left, continue heading downhill until reaching a footbridge in the bottom left hand corner of the field.

7. Turn left over the footbridge where you rejoin the 1066 Country Walk path for most of the way back, and there are sheep as far as the eye can see! Go across the field following the line of pylons until crossing a stile on the left. Then bear right across a field for a short distance to a stile next to a gate. Follow the path uphill, which soon becomes a hard track passing **Upper Brook House** on your right. The path zigzags up past **Brook Farm**, going through two gates next to cattle grids.

Brook Farm. Photo by Cheryl Wood.

8. Bear right after passing the entrance to **Brook Farm**, and after a short distance you will rejoin **Broad Street**. Ignoring the right turn to Snaylham, we leave the 1066 Country Walk path and continue for 300 yds back to the start.

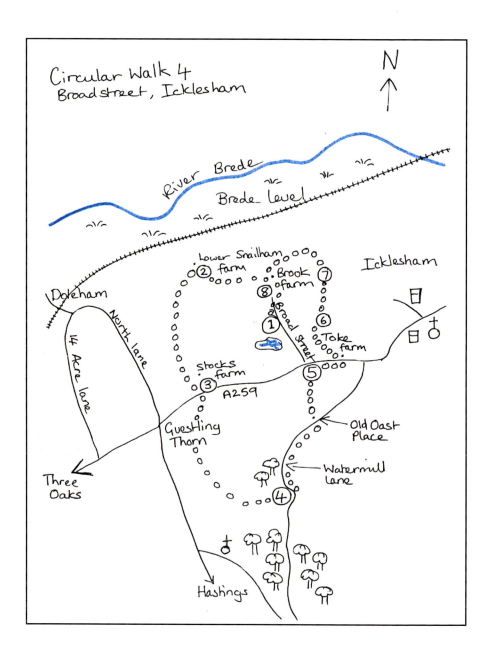

The Brede Valley.

CIRCULAR WALK 5: ICKLESHAM

A delightful 5 mile walk going through the tranquil Brede Valley, until picking up the 1066 Country Walk path just before halfway as it climbs up past the lost settlement of Iham into the lovely town of Winchelsea. You are rewarded with some great views across Pett Level to the sea, as the route gradually climbs up to the windmill, a well known local landmark, and returns through apple orchards back to the start.

- 5.00 miles ascent 299 ft descent 296 ft RATING 2 ... EASY/MODERATE
- 80% off road paths; 20% private/unmade roads/quiet lanes
- Suitable for walkers and dog walkers; however there are either sheep or cows in the majority of fields on this route!
- OS Explorer Map 124 Hastings & Bexhill
- Park in The Queens Head car park in Parsonage Lane, Icklesham, which is off the main A259 Hastings to Rye road
- Start ref: TQ 878165 Postcode: TN36 4BL
- Refreshments are available at the friendly New Inn pub halfway round in Winchelsea, or at The Queens Head at the finish
- Websites: www.winchelsea.net/visiting/welcome.htm

THE WALK

1. Go across the stile in the right hand corner of The Queens Head car park into a huge open field, and admire the glorious views over the Brede Valley towards Udimore, Winchelsea and the wind turbines on Romney Marsh in the distance. Follow the path as it quickly descends into the valley, dropping 140 ft in the opening ¼ mile, until reaching a gate beside a ditch. Go across the next four fields, all divided by gates and ditches, but keeping the main ditch on your left. You will pass a sheep wash, and may well see some swans and cygnets on this stretch. At the far end of the fields, take care crossing two high stiles which separate the Ore to Ashford **railway line**.

2. Now go over the footbridge ahead across the **River Brede**; then immediately bear right following the path to cross back over the **rail line** again. The path continues down a small bank to a stile, where you bear left onto a much wider bank with channels (known locally as sewers or drains) on either side. These have been dug over the centuries to drain farmland created by reclaiming the estuary. Continue straight ahead, always with a channel on your left, until reaching a gate beside **Icklesham pumping station**. Continue ahead for another 350 yds, ignoring the footbridge on your right, until reaching a footpath marker for Winchelsea as you enter a cornfield. You now have a channel on your right.

A swan and her cygnets.

3. Continue ahead across the cornfield until reaching a gate, with the **River Brede** now on your immediate left. Now follow a fairly indistinct path across a scrubby field to a gate across an earth bridge, with a channel running under it. You have a choice of footpaths here. Take the right hand path heading up to a gate in the top right hand corner of the field, with a line of tall trees ahead of you. As you go through the gate you will be joining the 1066 Country Walk, which will take you all the way back to the start. You now face a stiff, but undulating climb for the next ¼ mile as the path winds its way uphill giving you superb views of the Brede Valley.

A splendid view looking back into the Brede Valley.

After going through a gate at the top, you will see a bank across to your right. This used to be the site of a windmill moved from another location in the early 19th century, which was destroyed by the great storm of 1987. The windmill stood on the site of the Saxon church of St. Leonards, which was in the village of Iham ("high field") which pre-dated Winchelsea. Iham served a port established by the Saxons at the bottom of the hill below you, and was connected to the River Brede by St. Leonards Creek. Iham disappeared at the end of the 16th century. Continue across the field to a gate leading into **Mill Lane**. This marks the halfway point of our route.

4. Passing the attractive **Mill Farm House** on your left, with great views across to Rye, follow the lane for a short distance to its junction with the **A259**. Take care crossing over into **Mill Road** opposite, and then soon turn right into **Hiham Green**, which leads into **German Street** taking you through the centre of the delightful medieval town of **Winchelsea**, the smallest town in England. If you want to stop for refreshments then **The New Inn** is on your right; otherwise continue past the church of **St. Thomas The Martyr** and the spot where John Wesley preached his last open air sermon in 1790. The inimitable Spike Milligan is buried in the churchyard. As the road starts to bear right going out of Winchelsea, take care crossing over to the grass verge opposite next to what used to be the **West Wall** of St. John's Hospital, an almshouse for the poor. In the field ahead of you looking down across **Pewis Marsh** were the sites of two further hospitals Holy Rood and St. Bartholomew's.

5. Go across a rickety stile set into the wall, and then head across the field dropping down to a stile on your right. Cross a narrow path to the stile opposite, which leads you down to a stile next to a gate. Across on your left is **New Gate**, one of three surviving gates, which was built in circa 1330 and guarded the southern entrance into the town.

New Gate, Winchelsea.

Cross the stile and follow the path up the centre of this large field with **Wickham Manor Farm** on your right. Built in the 16th century, this was once owned by William Penn who founded Pennsylvania. Now owned by the National Trust, it is the centre of a 750 acre organic farm. Cross the stile and go over the private track to the stile opposite; then head uphill towards a stile in the top left hand corner of the field. From here you have great views across Pett Level to the sea. Cross the stile into the next field and continue until reaching a stile on your left. Bear right after crossing this into **Wickham Rock Lane**, and within 50 yds go through a gate on your left hand side.

6. Follow the path as it climbs uphill and bears round to the right until reaching a gateway into the next field. Ignore the permissive footpath sign to the left, and continue straight ahead crossing two stiles in quick succession into the next field. Go across this to a stile next to a gate, which rejoins **Wickham Rock Lane** at **Hogs Hill**. Follow the lane ahead for 150 yds passing **Windmill Cottage** on your left, before crossing a stile on your right. You now have a short climb up towards the old post **windmill** which has been restored and found a new use in the last 30 years, namely as a recording studio by Sir Paul McCartney! Take time when you have reached the top of the hill to enjoy the magnificent panoramic views. Follow the path downhill to a stile in the bottom right hand corner of the field, and cross over into **Windmill Lane**.

7. Turn right onto the lane, and within 50 yds go through a gate in the hedge on your right, still following the 1066 Country Walk signs. Follow the marked path through a number of apple orchards until going through a gate leading onto the private drive to **Manor Farm**. Turn right here and continue down the drive for 100 yds, before bearing left beside **Stable Cottage** and then following an enclosed path with orchards on your left. You will pass the churchyard of **All Saints & St. Nicholas Church, Icklesham**, which has a tall Norman tower and where there has been a place of worship since AD 722. The path emerges on **Workhouse Lane** opposite the village hall and recreation ground. Turn right and follow the lane for a short distance to its junction with the **A259**, passing **The Old School** on your left.

8. Take great care crossing this busy main road, as the view to your right is partially obscured by the bend, into **Parsonage Lane** opposite. **The Queen's Head pub** awaits you, just 100 yds further along the lane!

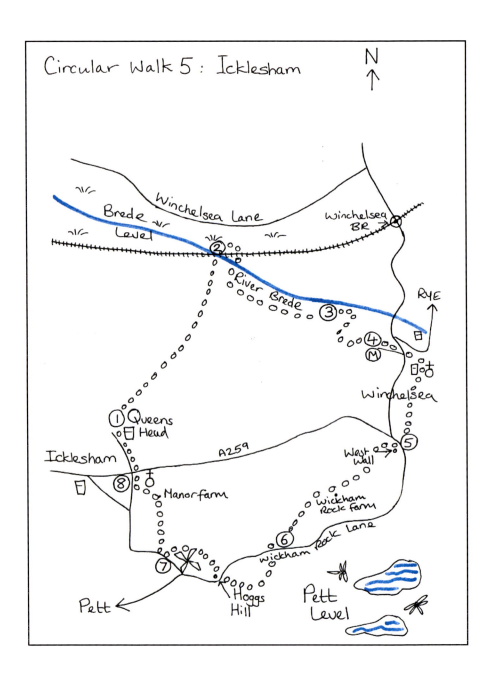

Poppies near Winchelsea Station.

CIRCULAR WALK 6: RYE

The easiest walk in the book by the proverbial country mile, where the only climbing involved is clambering over the odd stile! Starting at the 1066 Country Walk's finishing point at Gibbets Marsh, Rye you follow the National Cycle Network 2 route for just over half the 4.25 mile route towards Winchelsea, before heading back across fields to Rye with great views of the citadel and the windmill. There is a spectacular poppy field if you do this walk during June/July!

- 4.25 miles ascent 28 ft descent 33 ft RATING 1 .... EASY
- 35% off road paths; 40% off road hard track (rural); 22% quiet lanes; 3% main road (pavement)
- Suitable for walkers and dog walkers. This is almost a livestock free route apart from section 4 which has sheep in two fields, and cows sometimes in one field
- OS Explorer Map 125 Romney Marsh, Rye & Winchelsea
- Park in the Gibbets Marsh car park in Udimore Road, Rye
- Rye rail station, on the Ore – Ashford line, is 5 minutes walk from the start
- Start ref: TQ 916203 Postcode: TN31 7DW
- You are spoilt for choice regarding refreshments!, as previously stated in Stage

6: Icklesham to Rye
• Websites: www.visitrye.co.uk

THE WALK

1. The walk starts in **Gibbets Marsh car park** which marks the end of the 1066 Country walk. The windmill on the other side of the River Tillingham is a Grade 2 listed landmark, built in the same style as a smock mill, and also provides B&B accommodation! There has been a windmill on this site since the 15th century.

A "Gibbet" is a gallows-type structure from which the dead bodies of executed criminals – usually traitors, murderers, highwaymen and sheep rustlers – were hung on public display to act as a deterrent to others. In 1742 a certain John Breads, a local butcher, was imprisoned in Ypres Tower for the murder of the deputy mayor Allen Grebell in St. Mary's churchyard; apparently he had intended to kill the mayor so this was a case of mistaken identity! Breads was eventually hanged and his body left to rot in an iron cage on Gibbets Marsh for more than 20 years. Anyway that's enough local history...on with the walk! Turn left out of the car park entrance, and continue along the main road pavement (**B2089 Udimore Road**) past **Ashenden Road** for 150 yds until picking up the 1066 Country Walk signs on your left. For the next 1.25 miles this hard track follows the National Cycle Network 2 route, with **Cadborough Cliff** – a haven for wildlife, especially birds – on your right. After passing **Cadborough waterworks** and going through a gate, the path then narrows. Continue until reaching a cattle grid at the end of the track.

2. Continue ahead onto the delightfully named **Dumb Woman's Lane** (origin unknown!), and after 250 yds turn left into **Winchelsea Lane** still following the 1066 path and the NCN 2 route. The irrepressible Spike Milligan used to live further up the hill along Dumb Woman's Lane. Take care going over the **level crossing** at **Winchelsea Station**, and the lane now becomes **Station Road** as it winds its way towards Winchelsea. After passing two cottages on the left, you then pass **Newhouse pumping station** on your right. If you are doing this walk during June/July, then you must take the opportunity to admire the truly magnificent poppies in the field behind the pumping station! Shortly after this you will reach **Ferry Bridge** which crosses the **River Brede**. Apparently there were ferries operating from here until the early 1600s, going along the river which was ¼ mile wide as far as Brede Bridge. I am indebted to local resident John Chalkley who told me many interesting facts about the area whilst his wife Elizabeth made me some tea... John himself is quite a character, having been a Concorde pilot for some years and flying celebrities such as the Beatles across the Atlantic!

3. At **Ferry Bridge** we leave the 1066 path, and instead head back across country towards Rye with just under 2 miles to go. The town is dominated by the citadel, in particular St. Mary's Church. Go across the stile on your left, and follow a path across a cornfield into a gateway leading into another cornfield. Go across the centre of this field, and then over a footbridge. You have your first view of the windmill from here, as you follow a path across the centre of a rape field which can become quite overgrown during July/August. Aim for the top left hand corner of this huge field, where you then follow a channel, the **Padiam Sewer**, for a short distance before crossing a footbridge on your left.

4. Turn right and follow the raised bank across the centre of the next two fields, invariably containing sheep, linked by a footbridge. Then cross a stile next to a gate leading into a huge cornfield. Follow the path beside the channel, going through a number of gates until reaching a hard track. This last section of field usually has cows grazing in. Go through the last gate onto a hard track, which leads past **Dairy Cottage**, a farm building and several houses onto the **A259**.

Inquisitive calves just before the end of the walk!.

5. Turn left onto the main road pavement, and after 80 yds turn left again just before the **River Tillingham bridge**. Take care as the path crosses over the **railway line** back into **Gibbets Marsh** car park, which marks the finish of the 1066 Country Walk. And now it must be time for refreshments!

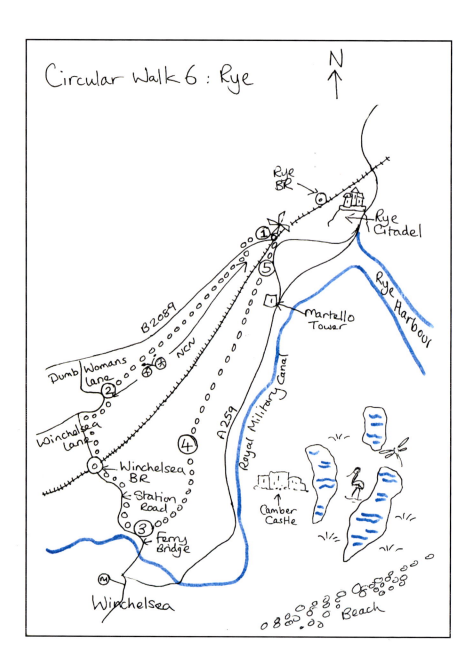

Rye.

The Author

Nick Brown

Being a keen runner and walker, I was delighted to fulfil a longstanding ambition in 2010 by having a book published of some of my favourite off-road routes in the 1066 area. **Walks in 1066 Country** has been very well received both locally and further afield (Australia incredibly!), and it has been very encouraging to receive all your kind comments. I have even bumped into people whilst out walking, who were carrying copies of the book .... and no they weren't lost! ... see **www.spanglefish.com/1066routes**

Nick Brown lives at Westfield, near Hastings and is a member of both Hastings Runners and Dulwich Runners. Aged 54, he has been running competitively and walking for 25 years. He won the local Beckley 10kms in both 2005 and 2006; has finished in the top 50 of the Hastings half-marathon (one of the most popular in the UK) on a number of occasions; and is captain of the Career Legal team which has been runner-up in the prestigious City of London 5kms race in 2006, 2007, 2009 and 2010. He recently organised the highly successful inaugural 1066 Relay, a 33.25 mile off road race over the 1066 Country Walk route which raised considerable money for local charities, and looks set to become an annual fixture now in the Sussex race calendar!

Walking South East

Walking South East is the brand name for the walking publications produced by Trailguides that cover the south eastern counties of England.

Being a small independent publisher, Trailguides specialises in the small, local guide written by the local author. To us this produces a guide that is user-friendly, easy to follow and provides as much information as possible, and all in an easily readable format. In essence, to increase the enjoyment of the walker and to showcase the very best of our landscape.

Our series of books explores the heritage of us all, and lets you see your region with new eyes. These books are written not just to take you on a walk, but also to investigate, explore and understand the objects, places and history that shaped not just the countryside but also the people of this corner of England.

If you have enjoyed following the routes in this guide, and want news and details of other publications that are being developed under the Walking South East label, then look at the company website **www.trailguides.co.uk**

Comments and, yes, criticisms are always welcomed especially if you discover a change to a route. Contact us by email via the website, or by post at Trailguides Limited, 35 Carmel Road South, Darlington, Co. Durham DL3 8DQ

Other walking books from Walking South East.
At the time of publication the following books are available, but with new titles being added regularly to our publication list keep checking our website.

East Sussex
Walks in 1066 Country
The 1066 Country Walk

Acknowledgements

• Principally I would like to thank my partner Helen Brown for her continuing support and encouragement. In addition she also came up trumps with her splendid "porkeroon" photo near Boreham Street on Stage 1!
• My best friend Martin Noakes, who has either walked or run round most of these routes with me!
• Again many thanks to Helen's oldest son Thomas for his ongoing help with the website, and for gradually improving my IT skills!
• A special word of thanks to Westfield artist Lorraine Ashley for her superb icons map of the 1066 Country Walk route at the front of the book. In addition she also drew all of the individual route maps.
• Finally I would like to thank Simon Mansfield, the creator of the Village Net which I have mentioned in section 5 of the book, for the incredible wealth of local historical information that he has kindly let me tap into!

DISCLAIMER

Whilst every care has been taken to ensure the accuracy of the route directions, the publishers cannot accept responsibility for errors or omissions, or for changes in details given. Like everything else the countryside changes; hedges and fences can be removed, field boundaries altered, footpaths rerouted etc. Also paths through woodland that are easy to run/walk on in dry conditions can become very greasy in wet weather. If you find any inaccuracies in either the text or the maps, then please contact the publishers as already suggested. Similarly whilst every effort has been made to advise walkers and runners of the likelihood of meeting sheep and particularly cows on each of these routes, there is always a chance that livestock may appear unexpectedly in a field and you should use your discretion if the need arises. However I have rarely encountered any problems in the 20 years plus that I have been running and walking off-road in the 1066 area, and sincerely hope that you will get as much pleasure from the beauty of the countryside as I have in compiling this book!

No guarantee whatsoever is provided by the author and/or Trailguides Limited, and no liability is accepted for any loss, damage or injury of any kind resulting from the use of this book, nor as a result of any defect or inaccuracy contained therein.

As with all outdoor activities, you and you alone are responsible for your safety and well-being.